A WEDDING IN THE FAMILY
MOTHERS TELL THEIR STORIES
OF JOY, CONFLICT AND LOSS

ANNETTE BYFORD

First published in 2019 by
Ortus Press, an imprint of Free Association Books

A CIP Catalogue of this book is available from
the British Library

ISBN: 978-1-91138-320-8

Typeset by
Typo•glyphix
www.typoglyphix.co.uk

Printed and bound in Great Britain

*To all the mothers who generously
shared their experiences with me*

Family life itself, that safest, most traditional of female choices, is not a sanctuary:

it is, perpetually, a dangerous place.

Margaret Drabble

Contents

PART I   **INTRODUCTION**   **1**

PART II **ANALYSIS OF INTERVIEWS**   **11**
             Notes on the Interviews   13

  1   Announcement of the Engagement and
      Setting of the Stage   21

  1.1 "How exciting!"   21
  1.2 A rock and a hard place: questions of maternal
       tiptoeing   34
  1.3 The other family   42
  1.4 "The wedding I never had"   51
  1.5 "You are not losing a daughter, you are gaining a son"...
       or are you?   58

  2   Wedding Preparations: the Middle Stage   65

  2.1 Transitions   67
  2.2 Hostess or guest?   69
  2.3 The guest list: who is invited and who does the
       inviting?   77
  2.4 The other family   84
  2.5 Maternal tiptoeing continued and the generous and
       the not so generous child   96
  2.6 Memories of "easier love"   105

CONTENTS

2.7 THE dress   107

2.8 "I've got a life too"   114

3 The Big Day   117

3.1 Hostess or special guest revisited   121

3.2 Getting ready on the day and THE dress
     revisited   128

3.3 The other family and other territorial issues   133

3.4 Choreography of the day: walking down the aisle,
     speeches and seating plans   141

3.5 Special moments and making memories   151

4 Time Travel   157

PART III SUMMARY AND CONCLUSION   **179**

PART I
INTRODUCTION

My daughter got married a couple of years ago. There was period of about a year between her engagement and the wedding during which we all seemed to enter a parallel universe, the rules of which were confusing and strange to me. I was not entirely sure that I understood what exactly was expected of me, but at the same time it was clear that it was possible to get something "wrong". I spoke a great deal with other women in my situation and realised that there was nothing unusual about my own experience and that many other women shared the slight sense of bewilderment around this event and their own reaction to it. Nearly all the women I spoke with informally referred to a sense of confusion around the "rules" of what was expected of them and of a sense of surprise at the strength of feelings, whether positive or negative, happy or sad, excited or disappointed, aroused by various aspects of the wedding and its unfolding preparations. A formulation I often heard and which seemed to sum up this slightly bewildered, at times amused, at times exasperated, surprise was "What was *that* all about?" regarding their own reactions and those of people closely involved. This is broadly speaking the question this book is concerned with: what IS it indeed about and what are the reasons for our own reactions in the context of weddings that seem to take us by surprise?

Participants of weddings agree that already the build-up to a wedding tends to turn into an experience that is characterised by strong emotions and unexpected pressures and tensions. Most people have tales to tell about friends and family reacting to seemingly innocuous aspects of the planning with an intensity which does not always make immediate sense to the observer or even to the people having the reactions. Old family conflicts that had been long forgotten may resurface. Emotions may run high and sometimes it seems as if the prospect of the wedding puts a magnifying glass to existing relationships, styles of interaction and communication.

In my conversations with mothers of brides and grooms, at first informally and then formally in a series of interviews which form the main part of this book, I noticed how being in the inner circle of a wedding gives you access to a world that you may not have been aware of and that may not even have held any particular interest for you. It is like buying a house or having a baby, taking a child to university or moving an elderly parent from their house to a different smaller residence, or losing a parent: all these are different rites of passage in a person's or a family's life. You are aware other people around you are going through this and have been going through this, but you only get access to the more intimate details when it is your turn. Then you are welcomed into a community which is eager to talk and share its experience. Whilst the weddings I heard about were different, and there were tales of easy and not so easy weddings, certain themes began to emerge that seemed present for nearly every woman I spoke with. Whichever way a particular wedding and its preparation unfolded, there were certain areas that practically lit up when we approached them. All mothers agreed the wedding was about the young couple making a commitment to each other and the wedding was going to be a public celebration of that. However, the wedding also brought into view a complicated network of other relationships, some of them reaching far back like the earlier relationship between mother and child, but also between mothers and their own brothers, sisters, parents and friends. Others were relatively new, like the relationship with the new son-in-law or daughter-in-law and with their respective families. Clearly all of them were emotionally charged and not all of them uncomplicated by any means. Past, present and future were going to come together in one big party!

What complicates things further it seems is the fact that the rules of the game have changed. If even a generation ago the expectations about how to conduct a wedding were shared widely and a protocol existed that was on the whole observed, such as expectations that governed which family was to host and finance the wedding and which roles various members of the families took, this is not the case anymore. Mothers were often a bit at a loss to know quite what they were expected or indeed allowed to do. Very few of the mothers expected to be in charge of the wedding (many of them had already opted out of a formal wedding for themselves), but where there may have been either relief or to the contrary, perhaps disappointment at their diminished role, what I found more often was confusion and a fear of getting something wrong. It was not immediately clear why this fear was quite so strong and why the consequences of getting it wrong took on such a heavy weight.

The rollercoaster that precedes a wedding forms part of popular folklore; wedding stories are everywhere: in magazines, on TV and in films. TV reality shows such as "Don't tell the bride" are frequently repeated and you could watch an episode every day of the week, if you wanted to. The premise of this series is interesting, in that it plays over and over again with the theme of expectations, disappointed and/or fulfilled, involving a whole cast of family and friends trying to make this a fairy-tale wedding that will make the bride happy. As observers, we are invited to enjoy the potential for disaster and then in the end its resolution. Whole magazines are devoted to the preparation for the big day and weddings are becoming bigger and more expensive, driven by an ever-growing industry.

However, when I started looking for more systematic research into the subject, I was surprised to find very little. Psychological exploration of processes involved in families and their experiences of weddings are virtually non-existent, whilst on the other hand pop psychology advice in magazines and websites on how to handle the stress of weddings is extensive. In this advice the idea of the perfect wedding day is essentially confirmed: if only certain rules are observed, then there will not be any conflict nor will there be any difficult feelings. It will indeed all be perfect.

Is this really on offer though? With the average wedding now costing £30,000 and the wedding industry creating ever more elaborate suggestions about what has to be part of a successful wedding event, the pressures on the couple and their families are huge. The cultural fantasy of the dream wedding, a mixture of tradition, celebrity and fairy-tale imagery, encouraged and sold by the wedding industry, leaves families struggling with a potential clash between expectation and reality.

Each family also has their own specific potential for such a clash between fantasy and reality: weddings do not just create expectations about how relationships in the family of origin *should* be and *should* have been, but also put the spotlight on what they *are* like and have been like in reality. Daughters as brides are supposed to be beautiful. Fathers of the bride are supposed to say wonderful things about their daughter in their speech and mean it and be moved and proud when walking her down the aisle. Mothers of the bride are supposed to be close to their daughter in the preparation for the day and are expected to burst into tears at the sight of her in her wedding dress. Both parental couples are supposed to still be married to each other and to get on with each other. Bride and groom are supposed to be close to their family of origin and proud of them, yet get on well with their new in-laws. Parents are supposed to be happy with their new son-in-law or daughter-in-law. Everybody is supposed to be excited during the preparations and happy on the day. If this is not so, then the clash between dream and reality becomes repeatedly visible in the preparations. It may highlight fault-lines in a family that have been hidden or ignored for a long time and force the participants to face painful interruptions of illusion and denial.

This book looks mainly, though not exclusively, at Western weddings which follow or at least are loosely based on rituals in the Christian tradition. In this tradition there is a focus on the couple, with particular emphasis on the role of the bride. In other cultures the particulars of the ritual differ; however there seem to be core components of the ritual that are very similar across cultures.

Whatever the cultural background and however traditional or indeed unusual a chosen wedding ceremony and celebration turns out to be, it seems impossible for all participants not to at least be aware of the traditional format and implicitly refer to it in some form. Couples may pick and mix in their choice of ritual, but in this process there remains the idea of a "proper" way to marry as a point of reference. The negotiations around this allow the observer an insight into what the couple imagine and display about their own relationship with each other: rituals put relationships into sharp focus and they allow and demand decisions around this display. Is the bride taking on the groom's name? Is she going to speak at the wedding? What is the narrative around the proposal? Who does the wedding work in the planning? It is however not just the couple relationship that becomes visible, but relational boundaries with family and friends are reconstructed in a series of decisions around inclusion and exclusion: who knows about the proposal? Are the parents involved in the proposal ritual and why? Where is the wedding being held? Who is going to be invited and who does the inviting? Who is going to perform a traditional role at the wedding, such as the father of the bride giving her away, making a speech? How are the parents financially and practically involved? Whose feelings are being considered?

The mix and match process of planning and then performing a wedding allows us also an insight into the rules of engagement between two sets of families. Beyond that they are showing us something about how these families deal with potential clashes between a culturally created expectation and fantasy on the one hand and the reality of a particular family on the other hand. The wedding is like a snapshot showing us where all the participants stand at this moment in time.

It seemed very clear to me that the intensity of feelings that can be observed around weddings cannot be explained by this one moment in time, this one ceremony, this one party. For the mothers I spoke with, all the elements of the moment in time seem to gain their significance because they are pointing backwards and forwards. The wedding does not only celebrate the commitment of the couple to each other, but it makes a statement about what kind of a family this has been so far and what kind of a family it is going to be from now on. Past and future come together in the story of the day and its preparations.

Another way of saying this is to note that weddings are a major family rite of passage, indeed one of the few remaining rites of passage in Western societies, marking a transition both for the wedding couple and for their families and bringing with it layers of emotional significance.

In order to explore this I decided to conduct interviews with women whose children were going to get married, trying to find out what it had been like for them during the months before the wedding and then on the wedding day itself. I could have interviewed the wedding couples or indeed the fathers of the brides and grooms. However, not only do women still traditionally do the major part of the wedding preparation work, it also seemed to me that it is the mothers who are in the best position to tell me about this curious aspect of weddings that places them as a rite of passage at the centre of a process of change within a family. After all it is mothers who are often the keeper of family memories, allowing them to link this event with the past history of their family and making them aware of its potential to bring about and symbolise change.

Interviewees were recruited via an interview on local radio, a feature in a local newspaper, adverts on wedding forums, in wedding venues and via word of mouth. I ended up with a group of twenty-five women from different cultural backgrounds whose sons or daughters were getting married. About half of them were mothers of sons, half of them mothers of daughters. The wedding couples were in their mid-twenties to late thirties. All the weddings in this group were heterosexual weddings.

This reflects of course the dominant portrayal of weddings as heterosexual.[1]

Most of the mothers were at the early stage of wedding preparations no more than a couple of months after the announcement of the engagement. Each participant was interviewed three times: at the initial stage, at some stage in the middle of the preparation, and after the wedding had taken place. There was a small number of retrospective interviews (mothers of children whose weddings had already happened).

The summary and analysis of these interviews forms the core of the book with the rhythm of the interviews also providing a structure. There is the stage when the engagement has been announced and the mothers talk about their first reactions to this announcement and their initial imaginings about the forthcoming event. We meet the same mothers again nearer the wedding when practical preparations have started in earnest and they have more of a sense of whether initial hopes and fears have materialised. The last interviews take place after the wedding, bringing the wedding stories to their conclusion.

The book then looks at some of these women in more detail and traces how their experience of the wedding fits their own life story and the coping strategies that they have used throughout their lives.

---

1 Gay weddings may follow the imagery and rituals of straight weddings. I would expect there however to be some significant differences in certain aspects. Not only would there be a flexibility regarding the gender specific role restrictions of the straight wedding, they are also more likely to be more strongly determined by the couple's choices regarding the celebration with neither family having a stronger traditional claim to involvement. The "difference" that is at the core of the gay wedding may allow both families a safer distance from expectations, as these expectations have been challenged more profoundly at an earlier stage. This would however be the subject of a different study.

A final chapter draws together the themes established and explores the question posed in the introduction: what is it indeed all about? Drawing from psychology, psychotherapy and family therapy it suggests reasons why we react so strongly to so many aspects of weddings, and what weddings mean for the families involved in them.

PART II
ANALYSIS OF INTERVIEWS

Notes on the Interviews

I spent over one hundred hours talking with women who had responded to my advert and had volunteered to be interviewed. Some came to me, some invited me to their houses. Each of those interviews allowed me an insight into this particular chapter of these women's lives, and often a lot more became visible than just the story of the wedding in question. The two following brief summaries may give an idea of the atmosphere and flavour of such interviews and, of course, how much they differ from each other.

Michele

Michele had agreed to be interviewed following her son's engagement. She seemed shy when she opened the door and started apologising about the state of the lounge and the presence of the dog. While she was making coffee for us in the kitchen, I set up my recorder and looked around: a family room, various pictures of children, young adults and, quite prominently, a picture of an older couple, probably her parents I guessed, the grandparents of the bride. During the interview Michele got up a couple of times and pointed out somebody on the photos. When she talked about her mother who figured quite prominently in her account of how she felt about the coming wedding, she actually brought the photo to the table, so I could have a good look, left it for a little while and then put it back in its place. She told me about her own wedding and how her mother's domineering and difficult behaviour overshadowed everything. She does not remember having any particular influence on what her own wedding was like, but recalls worrying about not asking for too much certainly not for anything her mother would disapprove of. Even so, something must have happened that displeased her mother on the wedding day, because she refused to speak with her daughter for several months after the wedding. Michele is not entirely sure to this day what it was that upset her mother. She thinks it may have been something to do with whether the deceased grandparents in each family were mentioned equally in her husband's speech. She never questioned it. Michele has clearly learned how to keep a low profile, how to avoid conflict, how to put her own needs last.

The coming wedding re-triggers all of this. There is no doubt that her daughter and particularly her new son-in-law are making an effort to get her involved in the wedding preparations, but Michele's main anxiety around the wedding is still whether her own mother will spoil the wedding, and Michele's own needs, or indeed her feelings regarding the wedding, are hardly visible.

> "There is a shadow over it and that is my mum, she can get very passionate about things... she has ideas... I get invited to things [by her daughter] and she [mother] does not, and that casts a little grey shadow over everything... I try to take a step back. Now I need to get my own outfit. I don't really want to go with her [mother]. It puts a bit of a downer on things. It will all centre around my mum again."

Michele does not really allow herself to figure: her mother has to be at the centre of things and the safest way to deal with that is for Michele to disappear. What was perhaps a necessary strategy with her mother when Michele was younger has now extended to dealing with other people and emotionally charged events.

> "It is not really important how I feel. I would not want to burden them with it."

In her dealing with the impact and challenge of the wedding she uses strategies she learned a long time ago: keeping a low profile and stepping into the background.

However, when I meet her several months later, quite close to the wedding, she shows me her dress, chosen for her by her daughter: a long, dramatic, bright red dress. She is clearly anxious about this, but there is no doubt she <u>will</u> be visible at the wedding!

Rebecca

Rebecca is a potter: she shows me her studio, but I would have guessed what she does from one glance at her garden, kitchen, sitting room. There are pots and bowls and vases in flamboyant colours displayed in every available bit of space. Often there is a cat sleeping peacefully and decoratively next to one of these pieces of pottery. Rebecca has nine cats, all of them strays. She introduces me to some members of her family: her husband, three sons and a daughter, and to various cats, pushing them off the sofa unceremoniously before we settle for the interview. I notice that she leaves the door open and I can hear members of her family chatting, occasionally somebody comes in, occasionally she will call out for one of them if she is not entirely sure about an answer in our interview. The atmosphere is relaxed, a family living in creative chaos.

I can't help noticing though that the door stays open throughout the interview and wonder how that will make it possible for Rebecca to reflect openly on any aspects of this wedding that may not be entirely uncomplicated. But there is nothing uncomplicated about it in her account, nothing at all. Her own feelings about the wedding are downplayed throughout:

> *"Weddings aren't important. They'll tell us what they want ... What you yourself want is irrelevant."*

She does not admit to any feelings of loss even though her daughter is likely to settle abroad:

> *"They walk away, that's parenting. I might want to see more of them. But that would be at a cost to them, they are what they are. I don't mind, I really don't."*

She cannot imagine that there may be the possibility of any competition or jealousy with the other family:

> *"It's not a competition, the more people there are to support them the better."*

Yet repeatedly she compares her family to other families, spending less, not behaving in a "crazy" way around weddings, "like some", neatly shifting the competition towards herself and "some".

She describes the possibility of her mother-in-law moving in with them and when I ask how she feels about that, her response is:

> *"She is my husband's mother, that's it. It's family, isn't it?"*

as if that answered the question about how she feels about it.

The interview ends on

> *"We are very lucky aren't we?"*

with not a hint of anything that could be seen as disharmony. Maybe that is what it is, maybe this is a very open, healthy and happy family. Yet this is the only interviewee who has not allowed herself a confidential space where anything could be explored, literally by leaving the door open, psychologically by not allowing herself to explore any of the questions asked. As if "being lucky" could not also entail the odd not-so-easy feeling. Only later do I find out that the daughter who is going to get married is actually her husband's daughter from his first marriage. She does not mention that at all when going through her family tree, when this kind of information may have easily been offered. It is as if nothing that may interrupt and disturb the image of the perfect family is allowed to be acknowledged.

It is easily visible in both those interviews that information does not only lie in what is said, but also in what context it is said, sometimes even in what is not said. Themes that turn up in one context may be recalled and replayed again, like a leitmotif in a piece of music. As a psychotherapist I am used to listening to stories and observing interactions, always listening to those emotional leitmotifs. However, I was not these mothers' psychotherapist and they had not given me permission to interpret what I heard in the same way I might do in the consulting room.

So I had to be careful as to how far I was going to interpret the material given to me in these interviews. I have also been mindful that I have been entrusted with highly personal and at times quite sensitive material so, whilst all the quotes from the interviews are verbatim, I have taken care to anonymise any potentially identifying information. Names of course have been changed but, beyond that, biographical details have been changed as far as possible, short of making the information meaningless. This goes for the two interviews above as much as for all the contextual information surrounding all the interview quotes which form a major part of the next chapters. The women may recognise themselves, but nobody else should.

Over one hundred hours of taped interviews tell many different stories, variously entertaining, moving, upsetting, infuriating and uplifting. Of course, each woman's experience is unique and set in the unique context of her family past and present. Culturally different backgrounds create very different contexts and formats for weddings. However, there are also themes emerging that link these experiences and give them commonly shared areas which crop up in all of these interviews. It is these shared areas that I am focusing my analysis on, rather than the individual stories or indeed the different cultural backgrounds. Only the last chapter returns to individual stories again, focusing on how individual women dealt with this life event, given their individual life stories.

It is important to remember that each woman who took part in these interviews had volunteered to do so. Some of them just said they found the study "interesting" and "would be happy to help", yet some were also able to explore further what had led them to do so. Several of them expressed a wish to use the interview to think a bit about what was happening to them around their child's wedding and welcomed the opportunity to talk about it with a stranger. The majority of them, even if they had not been aware of this as a motivation at the beginning, described the interview as useful, helpful, "it really made me think", "so interesting to look at it from a bit of a distance". In the second and third round of interviews many of them said that they had been looking forward to meeting again, as it gave them the opportunity to think again about what was happening to them and their families.

On the other hand there was also the aspect of presenting themselves and their family to the outside world, regarding their handling of an event as public, and yet as intimate, as a wedding and its preparation can be: the wish to be seen as coping well was very visible, to be seen as being relaxed about the forthcoming event, as living in a close and conflict-free relationship with their child, essentially as being good mothers and good future mothers-in-law. This was sometimes in conflict with the wish to explore, reflect and be open about less easy and more ambivalent feelings around this complicated event.

The first interviews were conducted following the announcement of the engagement, early on in the process, when first reactions to the news and early fantasies, fears and hopes about the wedding dominated the conversation. There may be an early flutter of planning or even a rush towards it, but for most women the wedding is still quite far ahead. Themes are emerging quite quickly though and consistently throughout the interviews. For each woman this creates a baseline of what she might hope for and what she is worried about. The second interviews took place nearer the wedding, when preparations were well under way, and the themes of the early interviews were now developing and growing in detail. A last interview explored the experience of the wedding day as it had happened.

What became clear was that in spite of individual differences there were certain general themes that were emerging throughout all the interviews.

There was joy, excitement, pride, sometimes relief on seeing one's child settle and enter this new phase of adulthood. However there was no doubt about the powerful presence of other more complicated and troubled undercurrents, even at the very early stage. Loss, rivalry and feelings of exclusion became visible. Conflict in the family and between mother and child was experienced and feared. These themes develop throughout the interviews, but they appear right from the start in the first weeks and months after the engagement.

Chapter 1

Announcement of the Engagement and the Setting of the Stage

1.1 "How exciting!"

The rules governing the world of weddings are written borrowing from many contexts and discourses: contexts of tradition; contexts of a new wedding culture created by the wedding industry, popularised in magazines, films, television shows; contexts of dynamics between the members of particular families. They are often contradictory, leaving participants at times at a loss as to how to behave or indeed often feeling that they fail to live up to expectations created by those rules.

One rule is clear and may already create complicated feelings right at the beginning: the requested response of parents and friends to the announcement of the engagement is excitement and it very often is, sometimes to the participants' surprise. The near universal response to announcing one's child is getting married is "how exciting": you hear it and you find yourself saying it, even if weddings may not necessarily be something that you would expect to be particularly excited about.

The moment of the announcement of the engagement to the parents is often already heavily ritualised. Just as the engagement itself turns into a story that can be told and will be repeatedly told by the young couple to their family and friends and then in turn by the parents to their friends, forming the first act of this family's and this couple's wedding story, so does the moment of telling the parents. Engagements in the families in this project were announced after the proposal during a special visit to the parents; they were announced with both sets of parents present at the airport after a stay abroad; they were announced by both partners to their parents simultaneously in parallel phone calls, in WhatsApp conversations from abroad. In one case the proposal actually happened in the presence of the mother over Christmas dinner!

Most mothers can recall the scene in detail and take pleasure in telling it:

Michele's son proposed in front of the whole family over Christmas dinner and she shows me the photo of the occasion with everybody wearing Christmas paper hats. "It was quite emotional."

Jeanne's daughter told her parents at a small family gathering. "She said, 'I have got something important to tell you' and my immediate thought was: is there a baby on the way or is it marriage?... they showed us the ring. I do remember thinking, he must have done it in quite a formal way, that's quite sweet. I wanted to hug her straight away, I welled up."

Melanie remembers how they had no idea about her daughter's forthcoming engagement, but her other daughter knew that her future brother-in- law wanted to talk to their father before proposing to her sister. So the bride's sister tried to engineer an occasion where they would all be together and her father, who was not entirely predictable in his use of his mobile phone, would actually be reachable: "we were on this walk and my other daughter kept saying, 'Dad, Dad, put your mobile on,' and then he [groom] rang [to talk to the father prior to the engagement] ... and I got it then. [Laughs]".

Tina remembers the young couple turning up on the way back from their holiday. "They popped in on their way back from their holiday and told us and it was really lovely."

Ruth's daughter was also away on holiday when her boyfriend proposed: "She face-timed from her holiday at Christmas and everybody here was just screaming and shouting."

Sometimes the parents already know that the proposal is about to happen, either because there has been a formal talk with the father of the bride, or a more informal sharing of the plan for the proposal with either set of parents, or at times one parent or a sibling. The holding of the secret creates anticipation, and certainly the parents who knew something about the proposal in advance felt, not surprisingly, more involved and prepared for the moment of excitement. Here the notion of "generosity" makes an appearance for the first time: future sons-in-law, who chose to talk with the father of the bride or the parents of the bride before the proposal, are described as "generous". Whilst all mothers interviewed struggled with the description of this ritual, they felt genuinely pleased about what they experienced as an act of inclusion and a symbolic statement about the importance of their family link with their daughter and future son-in-law:

Melanie (mother of daughter) wonders, "did he ask for her father's permission? He may actually even have used the word permission, [laughs]", and she adds "It was such a charming thing, a sort of pre-proposal thing. I was most moved, it meant a huge amount" and later reference is made to the fact that the groom asks the bride's sister to help choose the engagement ring, "which was a great privilege".

Suzie (daughter) talks of the anxiety that is created by knowing about the forthcoming engagement, having to hold the secret: "what if I had inadvertently let something slip? It could have spoilt things. That was hard. But it was a lovely thing to talk about afterwards... having been part of it."

Moira (daughter) remembers the moment "he took us aside in the campervan, [laughs and indicates the size of the camper van], and said, 'I would like to tell you that I am going to ask C to marry me.'"

Marion (daughter) is amused when telling me about the moment: "As we were leaving he came bouncing down the stairs: don't tell M, but I am going to ask her to marry me and he wanted our... not permission, but he wanted us to know."

Irene who is very fond of her future son-in-law remembers "He said, 'I just wanted to ask you whether it's all right if I ask J to marry me.'"

What might have been seen by many mothers as a rather outdated or perhaps even politically incorrect ritual gains a surprising emotional significance in the experience of the mothers I interviewed: the scene is set for questions of feeling included or excluded, a question that will prove to be hugely important.

In some cultures the involvement of the family prior to the engagement may be even more pronounced. In Muslim families that follow religious and cultural traditions, the young couple may tell the parents of their intentions, but the parents are the ones who play a major part in the decision whether there will be a wedding. In Western families the couple will just tell the parents, or the future groom will inform the family of the bride of his intentions, maybe even in the traditional format of formally asking for her father's "permission". In traditional Muslim families it is the two sets of parents who will be actively involved in this process from the beginning. The parents and other members of the family of the groom will visit the family of the bride who then will agree or not agree to the marriage.

> *Nasreen has not met the man her daughter wishes to marry, but meets his family first, who ask for her agreement. "They all came, his family, brother, cousin, auntie, they all came... it is a big responsibility to make that decision, right or wrong... that's how it has been done all the time, it was right for me, though it is slowly changing."*

Clearly these different degrees of parental involvement are likely to influence the emotional dimension of the wedding for these mothers and they are much more concerned about the weight of their own decision.

> *Nasreen is still wondering whether she did the right thing when she agreed to her daughter's marriage and traces back all her emotions to the moment she gave her consent: "Did I do the right thing? Will she be happy? It happened the day I said yes, the rest is in slow motion."*

Either way excitement at this early stage is expected and often genuinely felt. When questioned as to what the excitement was actually about, different themes emerge. Not surprisingly a crucial factor is whether the choice of future son-in-law or daughter-in-law is approved of by the mothers in question. There are mothers who relate that they "adore" their son's or daughter's choice, or who are at least "very fond" of him or her and believe that their child has a good chance of happiness. These mothers declare themselves "delighted", "over the moon", "very pleased" about the newcomer to the family whom they "really, really like", "adore". Often they may in this context emphasise the fact that the newcomer to the family will fit in well with their own family or even add something, a theme that will become stronger as the interviews progress:

> *Fiona (daughter) declares herself: "over the moon, he is lovely, from the day I met him I knew he was right... He has a good understanding of our family. I can sit down with him quite comfortably when she is not around."*

> *Helen (son): "She (daughter-in-law) warms your heart, just seeing her makes me feel good. We are not a touchy family and it is lovely to see that side now in my son. She has brought a lot of emotionality into our family."*

In contrast to that, another group emphasises the fact that the partner is a good choice for their child and that the young couple are well matched and happy, but that their own relationship with him or her may be more distant or even problematic:

> *Barbara's son is going to marry a young woman she has not had a chance to get to know particularly well, as the couple live abroad: "Based on assumptions that you make about who your children get together with, I was hoping to like her straightaway, but I was disappointed. I'm not sure that I'll get on with her, but they are right together."*

> *Jane (daughter) says about her future son-in-law: "He is not an easy person to get to know, he is not socially very comfortable with people, a bit shy, difficult to get to know. It's going in the right direction, just taking a long time... but I think they stand a good chance of a happy marriage."*

A third group expresses direct misgivings about their child's choice, at times because their own relationship with the newcomer is remote or difficult, or because they have concerns for their child and what may lie ahead of them in this marriage:

> *Louise's son is going to marry a young woman who suffers from a chronic health condition: "There is ambivalence on my part given her health. He is shouldering a lot, he is carrying her and we help him to carry her."*

> *Diane does not get on well with her future daughter-in-law: "We always found her difficult right from the start. They get on well enough. There is a lack of warmth, she won't even come downstairs without him."*

> *Shirley has had serious misgivings about her daughter's choice of partner and finds the engagement when it is announced after a relatively short period of knowing each other very difficult. She is concerned about some aspects of the groom's past: "I cried a lot... I wasn't happy about it. I felt she had not known him long enough... I could not get to the bottom why his first marriage failed, why she left him. I don't like him on a gut level. He is not a warm person... We are a close family, we were hoping our daughter would marry somebody we would like and who would want to be in the family... He is stand-off-ish and we are a huggy family."*

Excitement for this latter group is not surprisingly overshadowed from the start, and a few express a distinct lack of excitement.

Sometimes, if there is excitement about the forthcoming wedding, this does not make immediate sense to the mother in question:

> *Marie (daughter) confesses never having been particularly interested in weddings as such: "I would have been happy, honestly, if they had just got married and told us, but now that I know there is going to*

be a wedding, I am strangely excited," and later: "I don't even like weddings particularly, so I don't really know why I am excited."

The overriding reason is the sense that a "proper" wedding is what their child would have wanted and that it seals an already existing commitment:

Melanie (daughter): "They are so right for each other and this seals it."

Gemma (daughter): "I was so pleased that it came from him. Seemed old fashioned to me that it happened like that. [Pause.] It was a relief: she would have wanted it like that."

Tricia (daughter): "She really deserves this [a wedding]. There have been some quite difficult times... He adores her: she deserves this."

Meriel (daughter): "This [wedding] is what she has wanted and it seems a weight has lifted off her."

Fiona (daughter): "She wants the whole thing and she deserves it."

It is interesting that all the above quotes come from mothers of daughters who believe that their daughter would have wanted a "proper" wedding.

Many of the mothers focus on the idea of the wedding as a "party", as a chance to celebrate and get family and friends together. On a deeper level there may also be a sense that this wedding provides the chance to get something right, maybe if there has been a difficult or disappointing wedding in the past or if life has been tough for a while prior to the engagement:

A WEDDING IN THE FAMILY

Angie's son had been together with his girlfriend for several years and then announced the engagement: "My first reaction was 'at last,' because I knew they had been talking about a life together and children. And then 'oh good: there is going to be a wedding!'"

Michele (son) has had a hard time over the last couple of years. The wedding is "something nice to look forward to."

Melanie (daughter) wonders: "It's really difficult: why am I happy about a wedding? I am thinking about them, the commitment is important to them, but also, it will be a lovely event for the family, a beautiful celebration."

Ruth (daughter) is delighted about everything as far as the forthcoming wedding is concerned. At last she will be able to answer her friends' questions: "It's a big thing with my friends. It's: 'Any news??' And now it's: 'Yeah, I've got a wedding.' At my time of life you want a wedding, maybe grandchildren later." She also has had a hard time in recent years with several bereavements in the family. The wedding feels like a well overdue happy family event "There is going to be a party, a chance to get the family together and it's not for a funeral this time."

This excitement however can become complicated fairly soon. There may be for the first time a heightened awareness of the "other" family. This after all is going to be an event that will involve two families, the bride's and the groom's. Were the other family equally pleased? There may even be the first emergence of a sense of competition or jealousy. Which parents were told first? Did one set give the right reaction in comparison to the other? What are their expectations like?

Jeanne's daughter announced the engagement at a small family gathering with both sets of parents present "[when the engagement was announced] I was very aware of his mum. I was delighted that she was happy too. She immediately reached for the tissues, we all hugged. I don't really know what my husband did. I was much more aware of her [other mother] than of him."

Meriel (daughter) wonders about the other family: "They went to his parents afterwards. We should have done something with his parents to celebrate the engagement I suppose, but it somehow did not happen... I am sure they are pleased I suppose."

Fiona (son) has rather unpleasant memories of the first contact with the other family shortly after the engagement: "They [future parents-in-law] rang a week after the engagement and asked how much money we would provide."

In fact, there is a question which emerges right at this early stage, namely which family is going to be the "dominant" family around this wedding. Which family is likely to "own" this wedding? This question will become louder as time goes on.

Gender lines still dominate the discussion and the first "excitement" is heavily influenced by this: the most straightforward excitement was expressed by mothers of daughters, particularly those mothers who saw the wedding announcement in the context of the couple being more part of their family than that of the groom and predicted that the other family would not to be too involved or interested in the wedding. In other words, they expected to be the dominant family:

Meriel (daughter): "I am sure they [the groom's parents] are pleased, but they are not that fussed about that sort of thing... We see more of him than they see of her."

Fiona (daughter): "His parents couldn't care less. His mother does not approve of big weddings. She won't want to see the dress. She won't be interested in any of that."

Tricia (daughter): "They [the groom's family] are a bit at arm's length."

Melanie (daughter): "They [the groom's family] have not seen the venue and it does not look like they are going to contribute."

Beverly (daughter): "They are quiet people, they won't mind not being too involved... He is close to them, but it is boy close, rather than girl close, [laughs] ... "

For some mothers of daughters at this stage there is also the prospect of doing something together with their daughter, imagining the planning of the day as something that may turn into a pleasant and playful confirmation of a mother/daughter bond:

Suzie says she talked about this with her daughter quite early on: "I have seen so many people have difficult times planning a wedding, so I said to her [her daughter]: 'let's just have fun.'"

Tricia (daughter) is imagining what things might be like in the build-up to the wedding and what about it she is looking forward to: "I think it is the excitement of organising it, how everything looks, getting the dress, keeping secrets, all the girlie stuff is really exciting... making lists... doing it with her."

Mothers of sons on the other hand were more likely to resign themselves to a slight bystander role from the start, even in some cases expressing relief at this permission to keep a less involved role. However, this can easily and quickly turn into resentment, when it is felt that the groom's family and even the groom are seen to be almost incidental to proceedings:

> Melanie, whose daughter is going to get married, compares it to the previous wedding of her son: "It did not feel the same at all and that surprises me, because I regard myself as a very modern woman. We just got totally caught up in the traditions of another family."

> Beverly is in the same position and also remembers it being very different when her son got married: "It was very different with my son: they did not want to talk about it [the wedding] for quite a while, totally different."

> Barbara's son says to her: "I just let her have what she wants." Her own attitude is mixed: "It's going to be quite a big wedding and it's all going to be over there. I'm not that fussed, maybe when I get there, I don't know how I'll feel. But of course, the mother of the groom, you don't have a job, I'll be hanging around."

It is when the prediction of involvement along gender lines is confused that the experience becomes particularly complicated. If the groom's family was, for whatever reason, seen to be more dominant or more in charge of the forthcoming wedding, this contributed to a more muted and complicated excitement in the mothers of the brides. It is as if the attitude of being "not that fussed" which is often expressed by mothers of grooms at least at this early stage, is not easily available to the mother of the bride in this situation. One mother of a bride describes the moment when she was told that the wedding was going to be held abroad, near the groom's parents, as a sudden collapse of excitement:

> Marie (daughter): "it felt like a burst balloon." "When I tell people about the wedding they say, 'oh, how exciting,' and then they ask,

'where is it going to be?' and I tell them, and you can see they are struggling to know what to say next, and I say, 'oh I don't really mind,' ... but I do."

So whilst excitement is expressed and indeed expected, excitement at the stage of the announcement of the engagement is already presented by many mothers as not at all straightforward. The nature of their relationship with their own child, their future son- or daughter-in-law, the other family, the choice of venue near either family, are all creating a context in which first reactions, feelings and thoughts are emerging.

Shirley puts it rather neatly: "Weddings... like having a baby. Everybody expects you to be joyful about it all of the time. It's the same with weddings, everybody expects you to be excited. But it's not necessarily like that, there may be other things under the surface."

So what are these "other things under the surface"?

1.2 A rock and a hard place: questions of maternal tiptoeing

In my attempt to recruit volunteer interviewees for this project I asked a local newspaper whether they would write a little feature about the project. It appeared under the title "Are you a monster-in-law?" It is as if the chances are quite high of getting something wrong in this process that turns sons and daughters into husbands and wives and mothers into mothers-in-law. Indeed could mothers turn into "monsters"?

Whatever the circumstances surrounding the original excitement, and whatever its quality, mothers describe the announcement of the engagement as a moment where often another question appears simultaneously for the first time: did I get it right? Whilst excitement is required, the question appears and will stay throughout the coming months: how much excitement is the right amount and what is the right quality of excitement?

Tricia receives a text from her daughter whilst with colleagues at work: "I got this text, he has just asked me to marry him and I rang her. I was very excited, but it was quite difficult, because I was with two other people." When meeting her daughter face to face later, "I said, 'I bet you, you phoned x [best friend] and I bet you, she just screamed.' ... The fact that her friend was able to do that, give her that excitement. I remember thinking, I wish I could be like that at the time. I wanted somebody to do that for her." She also wonders: "At the moment, because I have so much work on, there is this thing, I feel a bit guilty for not being there now and not being excited with her and might have taken the edge off the excitement."

Gemma thinks her daughter is disappointed with her parents' reaction: "She felt we weren't excited enough, she wanted more reference to it" and she is trying to make an effort: "our approach to marriage and weddings is different to theirs, but we have tried to create other opportunities to celebrate it again."

"Did I get it right?" This question sets the scene for an ongoing dynamic throughout the coming months. All the mothers questioned were aware from the announcement onwards that the forthcoming event would be challenging. Excitement is required, as described in the previous chapter. That much is clear, but how does that translate into levels of practical involvement? How much involvement is too much and how much is too little? Too much excitement and involvement, and you are in danger of being seen as interfering; too little, and you are in danger of being seen as not interested and involved enough. This dynamic is going to run and run.

Again, gender lines play a part in the expectation and management of "excitement" and involvement. Mothers are under more pressure to perform excitement on the one hand, but under equal pressure not to become too involved and thereby somehow the stereotypical interfering mother/mother-in-law. This is often experienced as an impossible double bind.

Fathers on the other hand are more often allowed a bemused distance. A wedding card I came across, depicting a young man showing off his hand with the wedding ring to his male friends who perform the excited admiration-of-the-ring routine, is funny for one reason only, namely that all the participants are male. Not only do male participants not need to show the same level of excitement; it would be funny if they did. This lets fathers off the hook for lengthy periods during the wedding preparations.

When women in the interviews at the very early stage after the engagement were talking about how they imagined the wedding preparations and the wedding to be and what their involvement in it might be like, anxieties surfaced very quickly. Mothers hoped to get this right, but their degrees of confidence that they would manage it varied considerably. Often at this stage advice is sought, websites are visited, wedding magazines bought and friends consulted.

References were made to their own weddings, previous weddings in the family and the quality of the relationship with the child who is going to get married. All of these may provide sources of anxiety or reassurance.

It is pre-existing patterns of relating to the child in question which are bound to play the biggest part in the anxious or optimistic anticipation of the time to come.

It was only those mothers of daughters who felt very sure of their relationship with their daughter, describing it as relatively conflict free and exceptionally close, who predicted at this stage that they could not imagine any problems around the wedding preparations. They tended to be very confident that they would plan this wedding together with their daughter:

> *Beverly (daughter) recounts the comment a wedding planner at one of the wedding fair venues made to her: "There are four people to be considered: first the bride, then the mother of the bride, then the father of the bride, because he pays for everything, then the groom, [laughs]."*

> *She is sure: "She [daughter] and I will be planning it together. We'll enjoy doing this together, pause, ... with W [groom] ... I have to be mindful that it is his wedding too ... but he does not want to be involved in the minutiae."*

These mothers however are in the minority, even at the beginning, and some of them were often mothers who described their daughter as the "easy child", with another more difficult sibling present in the family:

> *Beverly, who was earlier predicting an easy wedding and a pleasant time of preparation for it, describes her daughter as "on a scale [of difficulty as a teenager] of 1 to 10 she was about 3, her brother was about 10."*

> *Ruth similarly predicts an easy ride: "L [the daughter who is going to get married] is not going to be a bridezilla, my other daughter might be."*

Mothers of sons who did not predict any problem at this stage did so rather on the basis of their own slight detachment:

> *Isabelle's son has lived with his girlfriend for years: "I was not surprised. I got a call from him, 'I have something to tell you, we are getting married.' When he gave me the date I said: 'Is it a Saturday, as I had booked myself on a course?' My first thought was: 'what am I going to wear?' Apart from that I wasn't too bothered."*

None of this may of course be proven to be correct in the unfolding events of the wedding preparations.

In most of the early interviews however there is something in the air about the potential for getting it wrong. The interviews are full of maternal declarations that they do not want to interfere, that everything about the wedding is the young couple's choice. Several mothers are concerned that they do not want to be overbearing and overpowering:

> *Suzie (daughter): "I don't want to be the difficult one."*

> *Meriel (daughter): "I don't want to feel that I am dictating."*

> *Fiona (daughter): "I have to be careful not to be overbearing. I just get a bit over-enthusiastic."*

> *Tricia has previously been very concerned with not being excited enough: "... but it's her choice not mine... How much can I do without overstepping the mark, maybe step back a bit."*

Angie (son): "I find myself trying not to be over-involved, not to influence their decisions... I don't want to be greedy, [laughs]." She later talks about looking for a "middle place between being involved, but not over-involved."

Suzie (daughter) talks of the wedding marking "the transition to a new order: the level of diplomacy required is quite a challenge."

Shirley (daughter) is trying to find an acceptable position: "I feel so confused... I feel I have to pick my battles... it isn't up to me, but I want it to be up to me... I have to choose the things that I feel strongly about."

Mothers of sons tend to find the holding back easier at this stage, often commenting that after all it is going to be "her" (the bride's) day or predicting the mother-in-law to be in charge. They are however also more likely to express ambivalent or negative feelings directly and early on:

Diane is quite critical: "She [daughter-in-law] is going to have what she wants, he is going along with that and they are getting carried away with the whole thing."

Barbara (son) is talking about the wedding in a year's time: "There is a lot of planning already, it's been going on for ages. I find that really difficult. I don't mind a bit of luxury, but the amount of time it's already taken! She has her dress a year before the wedding. They sent us the seating plan already."

Louise (son) admits: "I have a certain ambivalence towards the whole thing, a big wedding, an expensive venue, a large guest list, the full works basically."

For many mothers of both daughters and sons, responding to what most of them describe as the challenge of the coming months, the fear of getting it wrong, whilst cheerfully downplayed at first by most, turns after further exploration into a sense of some danger: getting it wrong could have consequences which as yet are difficult for most women to describe. Descriptions emerge of the child in question as "scary" or the current situation as one that could potentially lead to a volatility resembling more a parent/adolescent or even parent /toddler interaction. These thoughts are in most cases laughed off at this early stage:

> Marion (daughter): "It's taken out of my hands. I thought we would do this together. But there are phone calls and texts, we have booked this, we have done that, we have bought this. And I think, oh right, I would have liked to be a bit more involved [laughs], but she has always been like that: with the Lego it was: go away, I want to do this by myself... I just hope we don't fall out on Christmas day talking about the wedding. We went on holiday together and there was a rule about the wedding: no talking! [Laughs.] Whenever we talk about it, it gets a bit bristly."

One mother declares herself "terrified" by her daughter's potential reactions:

> Gemma (daughter): "We are always terrified of her reaction. [Laughs.] Almost teenage way she may react... You can almost hear the door slamming, and you think, 'Oh god, I thought we got past all that.'"

Again and again mothers talk about having to be careful:

Sharon (daughter): "You have to be very careful not to upset her, she can run off shouting, she'll still do. I'll have to take a deep breath and say, 'oh, that's wonderful.'"

Sheila (daughter): "If I talked about it too much, she would interpret it as, you don't like him, so I had to be quite careful about the amount I said."

Marion (daughter): "You have to be so careful. My daughter was telling me she was going to wear this necklace, (which won't go with the dress), and I said, you can't wear that, and I saw B [husband] looking at me as if saying, back away! You have to be so careful!"

Another mother asks:

Melanie (daughter): "Why don't I just pick up the phone to ask them what they are expecting of me? I don't know why I don't. Pause. Something about being <u>so</u> afraid that whatever I say, something may be misinterpreted. [Laughs.] This goes back a long way. She is able to be critical of me in quite a cutting way."

There is a fear that "getting it wrong" may alienate the young couple. In fact, if there is going to be conflict about any aspect of the wedding, then this may drive a wedge between the mother and her child: loss becomes a possibility:

Diane (son) talks of an early disagreement about the distance between the wedding venue and the reception venue. "Everything was very difficult after that. It affected me a lot... it did put a lot of pressure on to our relationship."

Melanie goes further than that and describes the wedding of her daughter as a potential "tipping point". "I am wary how it will go beyond that." This leads to the story of her son who since his wedding has moved to live closer to his wife's family and has been submerged in this in-law-family. "She [the mother-in-law] takes the children to school every day, we visit two or three times a year."

There is something in the air about the contrast between the expected and actually felt excitement, between the wish to be accommodating, supportive and not interfering on the one hand and on the other hand the awareness that something could go wrong. It is clear that this feels dangerous in an as yet unspecified way. Melanie's last comment hints at what is at stake: not the wedding itself, but the future relationship with the young couple.

This leads to an emphasis on effort, caution and restraint, rather than a relaxed and confident attitude towards the forthcoming event and its preparation. While getting it right promises at least for mothers of daughters the prospect of some blissful girlie togetherness, getting it wrong could easily turn them into something that could be perceived as monstrous, the "monster-in-law" of the newspaper article. Will the "monster-in-law" be punished by her child withdrawing from her? No surprise that the task of diplomacy is a crucial and difficult one.

This theme will become stronger during the preparation stage.

1.3 The other family

The announcement of the engagement sets the scene for a new chapter in a family's life cycle and what becomes immediately clear is that the act of announcement is being played out at least twice: it involves at least two sets of families. This wedding will join together a couple, but it will also join together two families who will be involved in the upcoming event.

In their choice of announcement the young couple are consciously or inadvertently making the first statement regarding their positioning within these two sets of families and the mothers interviewed for this study were aware of this very early on. Which family hears first or may even have known of the proposal before the bride, and where and how do they hear? The groom may have talked with his own father or parents, but not with the father or parents of the bride, or vice versa; he may have involved his own or his bride's siblings; he may not have told either family, but discussed it with friends. The announcement of the engagement at one family's home on Christmas day will be experienced as having more significance than the phone call to the other family on the same day or the visit a couple of days later to the other family. The spontaneous phone call from daughter to mother tells of a different dynamic than the joint visit by the couple. The simultaneous phone calls by each partner to their set of parents or indeed the announcement when both sets of parents are present – all these staged and premeditated formats set the scene, and it is possible to speculate whether they predict something about the patterns evolving during later stages.

As with many other aspects of weddings, it is nearly impossible for the families involved not at least to refer implicitly to traditional expectations regarding this stage of the wedding story. Some mothers in the interviews were very much at ease with the idea of a traditional wedding, but even if some participants may feel ambivalent, if not highly critical of cultural wedding traditions, it is impossible for them to not know about them and notice deviations from or following of tradition. Fathers may be surprised by being asked for their daughter's hand in marriage, but there may also be a niggling feeling that something did not happen, if they were not. Mothers may not have any particular investment in "the dress" their daughter wears on the day and may in fact be quite appalled by the prospect of cost and symbolism, and yet they "know" the format and can be deeply upset when the mother/daughter bonding around choosing a dress is felt to be invaded by friends of the bride or by the inclusion of the future mother-in-law, or if they are even excluded all together. The bride's family is traditionally expected and may expect themselves still to be involved in the wedding and its preparations in a different way than the groom's family, or, if they don't, they may wonder what the other family expects. Will the family of the groom expect the family of the bride to pay, for example? Will the other family expect a church wedding or, to the contrary, not want one? Will they want all their relatives to be invited and what will these people be like? Either way, both families are aware from the moment of the engagement that the wedding will be a celebration that they will for the first time share with another family.

Whilst this fact is obvious from the moment of the announcement, mothers in the interviews at this first stage often had to be drawn to mention the other family directly at all. When they do talk about the other family however, it becomes clear that from the very start in nearly all mothers' eyes one family is likely to be more *dominant* than the other as far as this forthcoming wedding is concerned. At this stage the mothers are on the whole taking up one of the following positions:

- The mother who is interviewed may, in the way she tells the story, marginalise the other family as less close to the young couple or just not that interested in the wedding. This may later become a problem for the couple. However, at the announcement stage, mothers who described matters as above were quite happy with this state of affairs, in some cases displaying a slightly relieved to triumphant undercurrent. In fact, nearly without exception in this group, the families of the groom were described by the mothers of the brides as "not that interested". Sometimes reasons were given, such as the groom's family having expressed repeatedly a negative attitude to big weddings, and sometimes it was put in the context of the new couple being more part of their own family than of the groom's family:

> *Meriel (daughter): "I am sure they [the groom's parents] are pleased, but they are not that fussed about that sort of thing... We see more of him than they see of her."*

> *Tricia (daughter): "They [the groom's family] are a bit at arm's length."*

> *Melanie (daughter): "They have not seen the venue and it does not look like they are going to contribute."*

> *Meriel (daughter): "I don't think she would really be part of their family as such... It's boys and girls, isn't it?"*

> *Beverly (daughter): "They [the groom's family] are quiet people. They won't mind not being too involved... He is close to them, but it is boy close, rather than girl close, [laughs] ... She [daughter] likes them, but she finds them very reserved. It's different: much more regimented than her own family and her own family is so important to her."*

> *Fiona (daughter): "She [groom's mother] got married in registry office, she is not interested in big weddings. She may make remarks about the money spent, but then she may surprise us and want to be part of everything... I don't think so, [laughs]."*

In this context talk of the choice of venue confirms the notion of a dominant versus a less dominant and potentially marginalised family. First decisions about the choice of venue are very much something that is discussed early on after the engagement between the couple and the parents of the dominant family, often the family of the bride or even mainly between the bride and her mother. The dominant family are likely to be the family who will have the territorial advantage on the wedding day.

- The mother who is interviewed may see the other family as dominant. This may fit with traditional expectations around weddings: it is going be "the bride's day" and the parents of the groom often assume from the beginning a position of greater distance, often mixed with some relief that they will not have to be too involved in details, but also in some cases with resentment, if the other family's take on the wedding and the young couple is seen to be somehow problematic. Traditional rules make it easier for the parents of the groom to normalise this position regarding the other family being dominant around the wedding itself or indeed the engagement. If their son takes a slightly uninvolved attitude to the wedding, the parental stance can become colluding. Financial arrangements again tend to make it easier for the parents of the groom to keep a distance from excitement and involvement, though they may run the risk of breaking the excitement rule. This is something that may become a self-fulfilling prophecy or indeed may be unconsciously reinforced by the parents of the bride in the later stages. Mothers of grooms may declare themselves to be reasonably resigned to this, but resentment can already be seen at this early stage:

> Barbara's son is going to get married abroad where the parents of the bride are already heavily involved in preparing the

wedding, says: "It is going to be quite a big wedding, a whole social thing, not just family. I don't really want to have anything to do with the preparations."

Meriel (son) is not best pleased about the other family's approach: "Her [the bride's] family is very pushy. They want money, but not our opinions. They rang a week after the engagement and asked how much money we would provide."

Angie (son) observes: "The bride's family, they are the big players."

Diane (son) is of the same opinion: "I talked with friends: the ones who had boys, they all felt a bit left out."

As far as choice of venues is concerned, something that tends to be discussed early on, parents of the groom seem to be more often involved only at a later stage. In fact their definition of what being involved means varies slightly: mothers of grooms who declared themselves happy to be "involved" in the choice of venue tended to mean that they were shown the venue that had been chosen, whereas mothers of brides tended to interpret "involvement" as being more actively involved in "looking for" the venue:

Louise (son): "They found a venue and they took us to see it and we agreed it... they were not really asking our view, we were asked to rubberstamp it, but it was lovely, we were happy to do it."

Diane argued with her son about the choice of venue because of cost and location: "He was so upset with us that we did not go along with what they wanted... so after that we just enthused about the venue that he showed us."

Marion's son and daughter-in-law chose the venue without in any way consulting his parents. She remembers: "We were told what they had chosen, so we [she and her husband] just went there for a coffee one morning and we asked for a brochure."

Isabelle (son) is perfectly happy with proceedings: "They booked the registry office and a pub for afterwards. When they had done that, they rang us."

- A sub category are the cases where the family seen as dominant around the wedding is the groom's family, in conflict with Western tradition. There may be a variety of reasons for this: the groom's family may be dominant in social, educational and financial terms. They may be closer to the couple due to emotional, social or geographical reasons. Even if none of these factors are necessarily present or visible prior to the wedding, the manner of announcement as described above, the choice of venue in its geographical and cultural proximity to either set of parents, which tends to happen very early on, and possibly the type of ceremony, if there is a cultural or religious disparity, again set the scene right at the beginning in a powerful way. In this category feelings of rivalry and feeling threatened are more likely to be expressed and are more likely to lead to difficulties in the "managing" stage of the wedding story. Mothers of brides in this category are often struggling with a confusion regarding their lack of role, but this lack is experienced more acutely in this group and resentment sets in quite early:

Marie's daughter is getting married abroad at her husband's family home and she says with visible signs of distress: "the wedding would have been fine anywhere, but not at his parents."

Moira's daughter is also getting married near her future parents-in-law with whom there is already a lot of contact. She is more resigned to the situation: "She has been scooped up by his family. I am delighted for her, but... [laughs,] jealousy, yes there might be..." Later she says about the wedding that takes place in the groom's local church: "It is their local church... the mother of the groom had clearly played a huge part in her own daughter's wedding and is likely to play a huge role again... [laughs] ... she sings in the choir, she knows the people who do the flowers... There were times... K [daughter] kept checking whether I was ok about it."

Shirley's daughter is already living near her future in-laws and the wedding is going to take place there: "My daughter is getting married and it's his family who are there. A little bit of me feels not part of it at all. I don't feel I have a role, I am a special guest... She has always been independent and I am proud of that, but I am not really sure what my role is at all."

Nearly all of the mothers interviewed, whichever of the positions described above they occupied, were mothers of children who had been with their spouse-to-be for a considerable time prior to the engagement. The two families were therefore likely to have come across each other before. Statements about the other family tended to be cautious at this stage, concentrating on whether the other family was happy with the wedding and liked their new daughter/son-in-law, and whether relations between the young couple and their parents-in-law were likely to be easy or not. Little is said at this stage about the quality of the relationship between the two sets of parents. However, there was a general acknowledgement that the wedding would mark a change in that relationship. Again, mothers found this difficult to explain further. In fact, there was a considerable reluctance to talk much about the other family at all, unless prompted, as if this was spoiling the excitement of the early stage. Mothers of sons brought the other family in more, as their presence was clear as part of the wedding day, "her" (the bride's) day.

In a few exceptions where there had been more contact between the two families before, again the concept of generosity pops up: mothers tend to mention when the other woman who is more "in charge" of the wedding (financially, geographically, traditionally, perhaps as mother-of-the bride) reaches out ("I really appreciated when she..."). Equally some mothers in the "dominant" category would express a wish to get the other mother involved. Often, as we will see, there is a bad experience in the background of her having felt excluded at a previous wedding. This becomes more marked in the "managing" and "performing" stage where communication between the two families via the mothers has a substantial impact on the experience: positively, if reaching out takes place and is reciprocated, and negatively, if that is missing.

In this sample there were several mothers where there was a noticeable cultural difference between the two families that went beyond differences in internal family cultures. Several couples were of different nationalities, some weddings were held abroad, others were held in the UK but the other family was travelling here from their country of origin, some weddings were held across religious divides, or there were at least noticeable social and educational differences between the families. This poses a particular set of problems. At this early stage all participants are relatively restrained about this, although this may become more of an issue during preparations and on the day.

The question at this stage seems to be, for nearly all mothers, which family's "culture", internal or external, will shape the wedding day. In the background looms the bigger question: who will "own" this wedding and, more importantly, who will in the future "own" this couple? After all, from now on, there are two families with a claim of being "family" to this new couple in a way that would not have been so marked before. If the wedding and the way a mother may manage conflict and tension with her child without turning into a "monster" points towards the past and how this has been managed before in this particular family, then the presence of the new in-law family points towards the future. One mother used a description that struck me as capturing this dynamic very well: when talking about a previous wedding in the family which had been dominated by the bride's family, she follows this up by describing how this other family was now much more involved with the young couple and their children:

"We have become the Boxing Day family."

The real question then for all these mothers, when they are trying to adjust to the presence of the "other" family, is neatly encapsulated in this image: who is going to be the "Boxing Day family", now at this wedding, but, more importantly, in future years? The wedding with its ritual markers of "dominance" is seen as a predictor of things to come and that gives otherwise innocuous details a heavier weight and significance.

1.4 "The wedding I never had"

The wedding of a child may or may not be the first wedding in this family in this generation, but there is likely to have been another wedding in the mother's lifetime: her own wedding to the father of her child or to a previous partner. All mothers in this sample had got married at some stage in their life, some of them more than once. The wedding of their child brought back recollections of their own weddings. Some of them, particularly those who had got married relatively young, talked about traditional weddings with clear parental involvement, often the mother of the bride being in charge of organising the wedding, often a church wedding, often with a predominance of family among the guests. Others talked of relatively informal weddings, often registry office ceremonies, with a small guest list, entirely organised by the couple alone. Second weddings tended to differ from first weddings, particularly in the central role of the couple in organising the wedding. Nearly without exception the mothers commented on the change that they observed in the general expectation regarding size, cost and style of weddings these days in general and in their child's case in particular.

Some mothers had also experienced other family weddings before, weddings of nieces and nephews or even the wedding of another son or daughter. Again, this experience was naturally having an effect on their expectations and feelings around this forthcoming wedding.

Two particular themes emerged:

- The forthcoming wedding is seen as a chance to provide a kind of healing experience making up for painful and traumatic events. There may be memories of feeling powerless and out of control at one's own wedding, and the strong wish not to repeat this experience for one's own child. There may be a memory of feeling side-lined and excluded at another child's wedding and the wish to create a different experience for oneself. Either way, at the stage of the announcement of the engagement, there often is a strong emotional reaction, seeing this as a second chance to put something right, to repair a trauma. It is as if a badly healed scar that had been forgotten hurts again and there is strong hope that this time proper healing may take place:

> Melanie does not cherish the memories of her own wedding which she feels had very little to do with her own wishes: "I see my daughter do something that I made a mistake over. She is going to have the wedding I did not have. They are doing it right!"

> She remembers her son's wedding as "her day" (daughter-in-law's) and this wedding "will be different. I can feel it already".

> Fiona prepares for her daughter's wedding and thinks back to her son's wedding a couple of years ago: "[At son's wedding] the mother-in-law was in charge... this is going to be different." She also remembers her own wedding: "My mother didn't help at all, she wasn't really interested ... quite sad... and my dad was quite mean."

> Angie (son) also remembers her own wedding: "I felt a bit out of control, as if I had got on to a bandwagon. I don't want them to feel like that."

> Marion's own wedding was paid for by her parents: "My mother made me invite people." About her in-law she says: "I was not good enough for him, [father-in-law] made no effort initially."

> Michele (son) has very bad memories about her own wedding and particularly her mother's part in it: "Mum took over, she did

not have the wedding she wanted herself, [laughs]." Her mother did not speak with her for several months after her wedding: "I never quite figured out what exactly it was." In contrast to that she wants her son and daughter-in-law to have the wedding they want: "I don't feel it is important how I feel."

Sheila is not happy with her daughter's choice of partner, but she does remember her own parallel situation: her mother-in-law did not like her: "I know what it feels like. I can understand that."

Suzie (daughter) is aware of a previous wedding in the "other family" which upset the other mother-in-law: "it broke her heart and I really want her to feel involved this time." She also talks about her own wedding which was "awful": "this is a chance to prepare for a happy wedding."

Helen says about her own wedding: "It was a horrible day. Our parents did not get on with each other at all. I put a lot of energy into making it work, for nothing, a complete waste of time. This wedding [son] ... I am watching it holding my breath, it's like I am being given another chance."

- In contrast to that, it may be the case that the forthcoming wedding is experienced as a challenge to the mother's own values and traditions. The choice of church wedding or registry wedding can become problematic, if there is a leaning in the family to either. It can be just as challenging to consider a "mere" registry office wedding for your child if the church wedding has a spiritual or social meaning to the mother, as it is to consider a church wedding if the cultural and religious associations of it are alien or even objectionable to her. There may be a serious clash of religious and cultural traditions between the families. For most mothers in these interviews however it was the size of the planned wedding that was an issue. Weddings have become bigger and the planned weddings in this sample were bigger and more elaborate and expensive than the mothers' weddings, with only one exception. For some mothers this seemed a cause for slight bewilderment and an acknowledgement that this was "what they all seem to want these days". For some this was more of an issue. Several mothers named the aspect of consumerism and "waste" as something they were struggling with.

> Tricia (daughter): "I can't understand why you would want to spend loads of money on a dress you only wear once... I can't do waste and to me that would be quite wasteful. I grew up with never wasting stuff... but I want her wedding to be better than mine was..."

> Barbara (son): "I got married in blue cheesecloth, it was the seventies. I am finding these big weddings quite difficult."

> Moira (daughter): "It is exceptionally odd, the difference between weddings then and now."

> Ruth (daughter): "That side of things is crazy, the money bit. People spend so much on these weddings, the blingy aspect of it..."

> Isabelle (son): "It's gone backwards... It's obscene what people spend on weddings these days. Such a waste!"

> Jeanne(daughter): "Our approach to weddings is different to theirs, just as there was a difference between ours and our parents... we did not really have a particular conversation with our parents, it was just a private thing that you went and did... I have always worried about couples who invest so much in the marriage ceremony."

There was only one mother who was disappointed that her daughter planned a small wedding:

> *Shirley (daughter): "When you have a daughter, you have it in your mind's eye what the wedding is going to be like, through the years, dressing up boxes... We would like to give her the best wedding, we only have the one daughter."*
>
> *"I had in my head from when she was little... I had to relinquish some things."*

Other mothers were having difficulties with the emphasis on old traditions, particularly those which they saw to be confirming stereotypic clichés around the bride, experiencing it as a direct and offensive challenge to what they felt had been their own personal struggle as women to get past these stereotypic role restrictions:

> *Jeanne (daughter): "You would hope your daughter would be thinking very carefully about how they approach that kind of ritual, maybe it matters less now. For us it was all related to feminism. She [daughter] feels: 'feminism, you don't need that anymore.' It was almost clearer twenty to thirty years ago, which side of the fence you wanted to be on. Now it's [wedding] more about showing your status, that you are successful, which I personally don't like."*

Here the issue of the degree of difference that can be tolerated between mother and child, particularly between mother and daughter, comes into view: a difficult issue at the best of times, but symbolised in the negotiations and reactions around most aspects of the wedding.

> *Suzanne (daughter) names it clearly: "I don't know how I am supposed to react... It brings into focus the differences between you. It makes it visible."*

For those mothers on the other hand who at this early stage were predicting that the wedding and the planning of it would be relatively conflict free, there tends to be a comfortable match between mother's and child's choice of type of wedding, whether it is low key or a big wedding, not challenging the mother to deal with too much discrepancy between her own values and preferences and that of her child:

> *Isabelle's son is having a low-key registry office wedding and she is only told about the wedding a couple of months beforehand, once all arrangements have been made: "I didn't have time to get worked up about it... Actually, my own wedding wasn't that different, very low-key."*

> *Margaret is very comfortable with the planned low-key wedding. Her own was the same. She emphasises the continuity in family culture and values: "Weddings, they are all now crazy..., but we are not a family... compared to that... we like people to contribute not just with money, we did a lot ourselves. Her husband will walk her daughter "down the aisle, but we don't call it giving her away, we would not like that... we paid for all of it; it was nothing like some people. We probably are rather low on your financial scale, [laughs]."*

There is also already at this stage the suggestion that mothers of sons may on the whole manage to tolerate differences between their own ideas about the wedding and those of their child better, maybe because their role at the wedding keeps them at a socially acceptable larger distance from proceedings, but also because as mothers of sons they may be more used to the difference between themselves and their child and the potential for identification is accordingly lower. Whatever a mother feels about the difference between herself and her child, she will be confronted with it by the public nature of the wedding event, where something about her family and her relationship with her child will be displayed. At this early stage mothers are beginning to be aware of this.

1.5 "You are not losing a daughter, you are gaining a son" ... or are you?

A set piece for father of the bride speeches is the line about not losing a daughter but gaining a son. What is implied is the possibility of feelings of loss turned into a celebration of the opposite. Loss would have been visible in weddings of the past, when the bride may have married straight from living in the parental home. It may be a stark reality in cultures where the bride is joining the groom's family geographically and may move in with them, possibly far away from her parents and with little future contact. It may still be visible today in international weddings where the wedding seals the child's decision to stay with their new spouse in a country possibly far away from one set of parents.

In most cases in this sample of mothers the wedding did not introduce any change as dramatic as that. The young couples had nearly all lived together prior to the wedding; most mothers knew their new son-in-law or daughter-in-law relatively well and expected on the whole relations between them and the young couple to stay pretty much the same as they had been prior to the wedding.

And yet... all mothers had a sense that the wedding did indeed change something, often expressed positively as a confirmation of the commitment, as a "sealing" of something, as a statement of intent and a marker of another phase of the couple's life and the life of the family as a whole.

> Suzie (daughter): "Whatever one says, marriage makes something difficult... [laughs and corrects herself]: different."

The possibility of the couple starting a family of their own, making their parents into grandparents, is mentioned by several of the mothers in this sample. The focus for all the mothers at this early stage of hearing about the engagement is not the prospect of grandparenthood, but rather of change: for their child, but also for their relationship with their child and their child's relationship with the "other" family. This wedding and what it represents will change things: their family will not be the family any more that it once was.

Here anxieties do start to surface: mothers of sons do talk about the bride's day and her parents' dominant role in the wedding preparations, which leads to a number of them expressing thoughts about their own role beyond the day: whose wedding will this be and whose grandchildren will these be?, as we have already seen in their earlier thinking about "the other family":

> Melanie is preparing for her daughter's wedding and is thinking back to developments after her son's wedding some years ago: "I learned the hard way. After the wedding they moved where her family are. She [mother-in-law] is different from me: they voted for her and I came second."

> Helen (son) has always been worried about this: "The possibility that the daughter-in-law pulls your son away and only her family matters... I have always thought of that as a possibility, quite likely actually. I have seen neighbours watch the daughter-in-law push the pram past their house, three days visit at her own parents and a couple of hours at her parents-in-law."

Even if there are no anxieties regarding this, there is an awareness in a lot of the mothers that the wedding marks another step in a process that has been going on for some time: their child is drawing yet another boundary around their life where the parents become less central. This is after all a process that lies at the core of parenting, namely how to allow your child to become independent and to relinquish the central parental role. The mothers may well be absolutely supportive of this, some even relieved, but most of them know that here it is happening again and in a very public and ritualised way.

It is remarkable how many mothers talk about loss in these early interviews, not necessarily directly related to their child. Loss is a background to these conversations: the story of the relationship of the new couple may be told with losses as markers of time (a death of a mother, father, brother, a sister, a sister-in-law, a child). The first speculations about the guests lead straight to thoughts of family members who will not be there, relatives lost to death or estrangements, a child given away for adoption. It is as if loss is around, but cannot be precisely located in the context of this wedding. Some mothers are able to name this aspect directly, and when encouraged to look at other transitions in their relationship with their child over the years, some of them talk of the loss involved in facilitating their child's growing independence, away from a relationship where the mother is central to the child's life:

> Suzie (daughter) puts it very clearly: "They have been together for quite a while, they have been living together for quite a while, but this feels different. It feels: now she belongs to him more than to me. It is like the proper beginning of a new generation and I don't know yet what my place in the new order is going to be... knowing now her primary loyalty will be with him and probably has been for a while. And I think, but she is mine, I carried her for nine months, and then: no, she is not! And it's a mixture between exciting and sad."

> Sheila (daughter) describes her reaction on hearing the announcement in a not dissimilar way: "I was pleased. I knew it was coming, but I was sad at the same time, because it is a moment in time when your daughter moves further away from you... that's it, here we go... the boundaries are changing, not that you are not wanted any more, but your role is diminished a bit: it marks a change."

Fiona (daughter) whose daughter is still living at home: "She is worried about leaving home, because she does not want to leave me with my husband. She fears I will be lonely and to be honest I am absolutely dreading her going. We both know it will be hard, because we worry about each other ... R [son-in-law] says 'I don't know how you are going to leave your mother.' It helps to know that nobody apart from R is closer to her than I am."

Shirley reflects on the wedding of her daughter: "Inevitably when somebody gets married things change. It's not going to be the same... a new person in your family... unless it's somebody you really like, an extra son... inevitably it sets up a different kind of relationship. I did all my weeping and wailing behind closed doors, until, two days before the wedding, I was so upset with the whole thing, I cried most days, for no reason whatsoever, not even to do with the wedding."

"It's like a grieving process. It is like losing a daughter. You hope they will come back to you, but you have relinquished their future to a new dimension and it's going to change everything and that is part of life and that is how it should be. But that doesn't make it any easier."

Irene sees the wedding of her daughter as "the end of my responsibility, the end of my journey, financially it frees me, emotionally it frees me..." However: "After the engagement we were clearing out her flat, I felt moments of grief, losing her, letting go of her. It's like retirement, everybody says it's great, but you are at a loss."

Maggie's daughter lives near her new in-laws: "He is very close to his family. I feel she is being taken away from me a little bit... They are going to open a pub in the village where his mother lives and I think she will get involved in the business... when we go there, they [the young couple] normally arrange something together with his family, so I don't get my own time."

Diane: "They will be moving closer to her mother... I don't think she [daughter-in-law] is taking him away from me to become part of her family. I think she wants him just to herself."

Barbara's son is going to settle with his bride in another country where she comes from: "I am not likely to have them in this country, grandchildren... there is a sadness in it for me... I will just never get to know her very well."

Helen is on the whole very positive about her son's wedding, but nevertheless acknowledges: "There is relief, not so much my responsibility any more, it's now her turn [daughter-in-law], but here is also a feeling of sadness... you are certainly not the manager of everything any more, the one that knew about what was going on. I mean that finished a while ago, but now it is official."

Nasreen's daughter was still living at home prior to the wedding. Nasreen tells me how it all hit her one day when she was in the bathroom, where she was on her own for the first time during the short period of the engagement: "In that bathroom something hit me, my daughter will not be with me anymore, she is not going to be mine any more, leaving her room, leaving her smell behind, and I cried and cried."

Emily tells me of a dream she has during the early stages of the wedding preparations. In the dream she has lost her daughter and is looking for her. She wanders through a vast field where circus tents are being erected, but cannot find her daughter anywhere in the middle of all the busy circus attractions!

There is no doubt that in these early interviews any acknowledgement of the aspect of loss is experienced as slightly problematic. It may be experienced as in conflict with the excitement rule; it may be experienced as in conflict with the intention of being a good mother who can let her child go and encourage independence. Weddings are supposed to create excitement and joy and it is not so easy to admit to feelings of loss and experience of conflict. No doubt it may also just be very difficult for many of these mothers to hold conflicting feelings at the same time, to reflect on them and to admit them. Not surprisingly mothers who formed a close rapport in the interviews, who had created a confidential setting and who may have experience and practice in managing conflict in their lives and in their relationship with their child, were more able to approach this area. Some mothers were able to talk about both their excitement <u>and</u> their anxiety regarding the wedding, being quite comfortable with ambivalent feelings about the same event. Others could not entertain this possibility. We have already heard about the mother who made it virtually impossible for herself to say anything problematic, in leaving the door to the room in which we talked open to the rest of the house where her family moved about within earshot. The higher the pressure to present themselves and their families as conflict-free, the higher the pressure to see themselves and to be seen as either "not that fussed" or, on the other hand, completely "excited", the less reflection on ambivalent feelings was possible.

It will be interesting to see whether mothers who could reflect upon this had a different experience in the later stages of the wedding preparation from those for whom this was not possible early on.

Chapter 2

Wedding Preparations: the Middle Stage

The engagement sets the scene and, whilst at this stage a certain amount of planning and organising may have taken place, the majority of themes emerging from the early interviews so far have been about expectations, fears and hopes concerning the forthcoming wedding and the time leading up to it. For most women there is then a bit of a lull, given the length of the period between engagement and the actual wedding. Once wedding preparations have started in earnest however, the interviews begin to feel different. Things may not turn out quite as expected, people's own reactions may change, the rules of engagement certainly will have become clearer. Most interviews in this second stage took place a couple of months before the wedding, though some women stayed in touch and made contact at various stages in the build-up to the wedding, when they felt something had happened that may interest me or indeed struck them as interesting or perhaps puzzling.

Some of the themes from the first stage are continuing, some of the emphasis changes, and some new themes emerge. At the early stage after the engagement a lot of the reactions are, after all, based on still quite sparse information about the particulars of this wedding and therefore a lot of the feelings are anchored in anticipation and imagination. By now however preparations have moved on and the details become clearer. Whatever the mothers feared or wished for, a more specific shape is beginning to form in the details of the planned day and in the way they have been involved or not in its planning.

2.1 Transitions

Throughout the interviews at this stage of the wedding preparations there is a growing appreciation amongst the mothers I interviewed that they and their families are in a stage of transition that is symbolised and triggered by this wedding: something is changing or has changed a while ago and becomes visible now.

The biggest change is that their child is embarking on a life as husband or wife of their partner and possibly on a life as parents with a family of their own. That however also brings with it a change in the mother's role in her child's life:

Angie (son): "Tom in my mind is becoming a proper grown-up, a proper man with a family of his own. I have become aware that I am not the mum anymore who goes: 'I'll do that. Shall I do this? Have you done that? I've become aware of the separateness."

Suzie (daughter): "The girls grow, I have a bit of freedom too." "J [son-in-law] is already... what J wants is already more important than what I want, quite rightly."

Irene (daughter): "This is the end of my responsibility, the end of my journey. Financially it frees me, emotionally it frees me. Job done!"

Sheila (daughter): "The boundaries are changing, not that you are not wanted anymore, but your role is diminished a bit. It marks a change."

For most mothers this change is experienced as inevitable and in fact as a necessary step in the right direction for their child. There is a certain amount of uncertainty though regarding where exactly this change will leave them. The nostalgia and emotions when looking back on their lives as mothers so far are coupled with an anxiety when looking forward about where exactly the "new order", as one mother had called it, will leave them in this newly drawn map of relationships. Mothers feel that they are entering unchartered territory. The slightly odd aspect of this is that most of the mothers in my interview sample were in a situation where the relationship between their child and their partner had existed for a while, so in reality they had in fact been exploring this unchartered territory for some time. However, rituals are designed to compress a reality into a moment of carefully choreographed interactions in order to make its significance visible, and weddings do exactly that. In this phase of planning the wedding, the reality of what has been happening and is going to happen, as far as the mothers' own position in this changing family is concerned, is getting gradually clearer.

Not all mothers are aware of this. They may rather feel an unspecified restlessness that can either transport them into a frenzy of wedding preparations or into a preoccupation with the stress that can come along with that. The often unclear nature of their own role adds to this considerably. After all, weddings and what roles people play in them have changed.

Most mothers however know that their families and their relationship with their child are at a point of transition, symbolised by the wedding. There are a variety of factors that will underpin and influence the quality of the experience of transition for these mothers and I shall trace them throughout this chapter.

2.2 Hostess or guest?

At this stage of active preparation for the wedding there is one question that is now becoming louder and louder: what role am I supposed to be playing and what role might I <u>want</u> to play at my child's wedding? The answers are still at times not entirely clear. In fact, this may be the crucial question regarding not just the practicalities of the planning, but also the emotional significance of the details of the wedding as it is taking shape. It is less common these days that the parents of the bride, or even both sets of parents jointly, finance the wedding, so the economic basis for parents being the hosts of their children's wedding is shifting. If it was common, for example, in the last generation to be invited by the parents of the bride, it is now more often the couple who invite, either together with the parents or without any reference to the parents at all. Who is included or excluded on the invitation, like so many other details of the wedding, seems to follow a mix and match of traditions. It also however holds emotional significance and mirrors larger issues.

The parental invitation gives the mother of the bride a clear hostess role, and there were several mothers who still saw it like that in a quite straightforward sort of way. In the invitation by the couple the parental role is not specified. If the mother is not the hostess, then what is she?

Mothers who are safe and comfortable in the knowledge of being the hostess are, in this sample, in a minority. They tend to be the mother of the bride, following rules of tradition.

If, following the traditional format, the wedding is paid for by the bride's family, if the invitations are issued by the mother and father of the bride, if the wedding takes place at the bride's family home or nearby, then the mother's role is clear and she may just be aware of anxieties about the burden of responsibility for the day, and of course these are by no means small anxieties:

Suzie confesses to dreaming about the wedding and its preparation quite a lot. She says: "It's like doing Christmas dinner for the first time. You think you have everything ready and organised and then you realise you have forgotten the turkey!", adding, "It's like buying a really expensive car, driving it for a day and then driving it off a cliff."

Beverly confesses to not having "slept properly since it started... up at 4am and writing lists! There is just so much to do."

Nasreen (daughter) recalls: "all the time I was doing all this, holding responsibility for it all... I lost three stone!"

Alex (daughter) wonders: "What is my role? Just making sure that things are running smoothly... do we need to hire a van? How do we get things there? Who is helping with the lifting and carrying? ... Events manager, that's what I do... Others will get anxious about relationships and how people will get on, and I will think about how the crates get there, [laughs]."

However, this scenario where the mother is in the clear hostess role seems to be the exception.

Mothers of sons on the whole tend to be much less clear about their role and may, like Angie, declare themselves rather puzzled:

"I am not quite sure what the mother of the groom does, except be there. Essentially I am just a guest who is helping more than other guests."

Helen is trying to work it out: "We are more on the side-line, giving advice perhaps. I am not just another guest, I have got a role, but somewhere in the background."

For most mothers, of sons and daughters alike, there seemed to be a substantial amount of confusion around what their role would be in the preparation of the day and on the day itself. Indeed, the question seemed to be what role they were *allowed* to take up by their child:

> *Melanie (daughter) asks with an air of exasperation: "What am I supposed to be here? What am I supposed to do here?"*

If not hostess, what then is the mother's role? "A special guest" is a formulation that I heard a lot, and again some mothers were happy with that definition, even relieved that that was all that was required. Most of them struggled though, trying to define quite what the "special guest" role entailed, where on the scale from hostess to guest they were allowed to be or where they wished to be.

It seemed to me that this conflict was at the centre of a lot of the confusion, the manoeuvring between mothers and their child, the upsets and conflicts that took place. Why? Organising a wedding is a lot of work and being allowed to step back should have been perhaps easier than it turned out to be for many of them. Stepping back how far though?

More than anything I think that the question "Am I hostess or guest at my child's wedding?" re-kindles the question that would have been central to the mother-child relationship as it developed over the years: "Where am I on the journey from being hostess to guest in my child's life?" A hostess provides a place, food and care for her guests. She will be thinking about how to encourage social contacts, how to help people to feel at ease. She will be observing whether her guests are happy or need some help and she will see it as her responsibility that things work out smoothly. She may have to facilitate, to encourage, to comfort, to deal with conflicts, all in the hope that her guests will look back and feel they had a good time. There are clear overlaps between hosting and mothering, but of course the hostess role ends when the party is over: guests leave and the hostess' responsibility and involvement with them ceases. Being a mother does not have such clear indicators about when "the party is over". It presents mothers with the challenge to step back from the role of the "hostess", gradually, flexibly, appropriately and to become a "guest" in their child's life. Hopefully she will be a welcome guest, but certainly less central to her child's life, interacting with them on *their* territory, respecting *their* rules. A lot of this would have happened for all the women I interviewed long before the wedding, maybe to different degrees. However, a wedding as a major rite of passage for the young couple also highlights for the mother where she is currently positioned on this passage from hostess to guest and how happy or unhappy she is with this. In fact, the wedding may provide everybody with the opportunity to replay the transition process in fast-forward mode, allowing all the players to regress to earlier stages.

Whilst a wedding may seem to the mother like a last chance to regress, to recapture something about the maternal aspect of the hostess role, it may rather prove to be a time when she may have to deal with the reality of how important or unimportant a guest she really is at this time in her child's life.

One mother recalls how not only was she not the hostess, but she seriously wondered how special a guest she actually was. When transport arrangements from church to reception were being discussed, there was a rather tense moment:

> *"The person who nobody had thought about from here to church was me ... a lot of discussion about the bridesmaids... eventually I said something, 'I have got to get to the church too,' and somebody says, 'oh, I can pick you up with whoever else wants to be early.' I was feeling terribly left out..*

It becomes very clear in the way this episode is told, how hurt this mother was.

Many mothers, and particularly the mothers of daughters, described this as a difficult process: they were often confronted with, and at times surprised by, their own wish to be hostess, and were then shocked and hurt by feeling that they were not even being treated like a particularly special guest. Were the daughters afraid that mother's special guest status might be turned into a claim to be hostess again? Were the mothers trying to regain ground and influence in their adult child's life? There is no doubt that something sensitive and complicated is being acted out here:

> *Shirley's daughter is organising her own wedding without attempting to involve her mother very much at all. Shirley: "I don't feel I have a role. I am a special guest... They have always been independent and I am proud of that, but I am not really sure what my role is..." Later in the interview the same woman says, "I would happily organise their wedding, have them live round the corner, that's really what I want, and then I think, 'actually that wouldn't be right, they wouldn't be independent and they would be in my pockets, [laughs,] but a little bit of me..."*

This neatly encapsulates the conflict: she does want her daughters to be independent, for their sakes, and also for her own sake, not necessarily wanting her daughters "in her pockets", and yet "there is a small part of her" that would love to be the hostess at the wedding and allowed a stronger and more active part in her daughters' life.

Another mother, Sheila, says:

> *"I don't want to feel like a guest at my child's wedding, I want to be her mother."*

But what does that mean?

Helen can easily describe what she is not *on the day, namely hostess, nor is she dominant in any way. She finds the best formulation for herself for her role on the day: "I am M's Mum, not just his mother, but Mum," explaining that that confirms the emotional link more than anything else.*

For Shirley (daughter), on the other hand, her role as mother is far from clear: "We had a conversation, the four of us, 'what is the most important thing to you? What would you like to be in charge of?' I felt like saying I want to be in charge of everything, but of course that was not an option. [Laughs.] Up to then they were in complete control and we were just bystanders to turn up on the day. And I got very upset, that was not at all as I saw my role as mother of the bride, and I told them. I want to be in charge, I mean I want to be involved... if you are thinking of something, just run it by me..."

"I was so confused, I felt I had to pick my battles... it wasn't up to me, I wanted it to be up to me... I had to choose the things that I felt strongly about."

Is this wish to be in charge of things showing us the archetypal controlling mother of the bride? This mother is very aware that her wish to be in control is not necessarily right or justified, but she is aware that the wish still exists. She is very aware of her changing and diminishing role in her daughter's life:

"And that's how it should be, but it doesn't make it any easier."

It may be friends by now who play a much more important part in the wedding preparations than the mothers, again emphasising the shift from parent to peer that characterises adolescence and growing up, re-opening possible conflicts and feelings that were present then:

Melanie talks about her daughter's friends' involvement: "She says, 'don't worry about that, Mum. Susie, my friend, will do that.' That's when you say things you shouldn't [laughs]. I said, 'actually I would quite like the odd thing to do...' I am being told, 'don't worry about that, we've got it organised.' The official message was: 'Just enjoy it,' but underneath it seemed to say, 'no, you just mess it up, Mum, we can do it better,' [laughs]."

Even Suzie, who on the whole has an easy time and feels reasonably sure that she is the hostess on the day, identifies this as the area of conflict: "And then it is, 'ALL my friends say it is a really good idea on the day to have a person who everybody can go to, to be that person who is in charge, a sort of wedding planner.' I just thought: 'no!' and 'It used to be parents' friends who came to weddings, it is now only friends who daughter wants to be there.'"

Tricia confesses that she feels like a bit of a "bystander": "The bridesmaids seem to do most of it. It is very much shared out."

It seems that for most of the mothers their child's wedding brings back memories of the days of being the hostess to their son or daughter's childhood: being responsible for and in charge of what happens, planning, providing, organising, making things happen smoothly, soothing and energising, looking ahead and making sure that everything is safe and can be looked back on afterwards as a happy time. Maybe there were also years when being the hostess meant being appreciated for this "labour of love".

The prospect of the wedding brings back memories: is this a last chance to regress into this kind of dynamic? Is this indeed how it happened? Or was it never like that? Will it present them with an image of a much more complicated relationship with their child, then and now? The child envisaging the wedding is seeing an event that points forward to their future as a couple; the mother sees an event that points forward <u>and</u> backwards. She is inevitably led to remember and re-examine her relationship with her child as it has been over the years, the early years of "hostessing", just as much as the years of her child's journey into independence and the mother's becoming a "special guest". She also will engage in looking forward: where is she going to figure in her child's life from now on? The wedding and the negotiations around it are seen as giving the mother a taste of things to come. It is this quality of pointing backwards and forwards that make the wedding into a true rite of passage.

2.3 The guest list: who is invited and who does the inviting?

At this stage of the wedding preparations the question of who will be invited and who does the inviting is very much in people's minds. Here the question "who hosts this party?" is very visible. If you are a hostess, you are the one who invites the guests. The parental invitation is however not the norm anymore. I came across different formats of invitation, most of them still as paper invitations, but some just as email invitations or as part of specially created wedding websites. The traditional format sees the parents of the bride as the hosts:

Mr and Mrs X

Request the pleasure of your company
at the marriage of their daughter

Brides' name

To

Grooms' name

On date

At time

Location

Both sets of parents may invite:

> *Mr and Mrs X*
>
> *And Mr and Mrs Y*
>
> *Request the pleasure of your company*
>
> *At the marriage of*
>
> *Bride and groom*

There are then variations on this theme if either or both sets of parents are divorced, widowed or single parents. This does not change the basic message that it is the parents who issue the invitations.

It may however be the couple who invite, either on their own or together with their parents:

> *Bride and groom*
>
> *Invite you to their wedding*
>
> *On date*
>
> *At time*
>
> *Location*

The couple may include their parents on the invitation:

> *Bride and groom*
>
> *Together with their parents*
>
> *Mr and Mrs X and Mr and Mrs Y*
>
> *Invite you to the wedding*

Sometimes the parents are not named, sometimes the formulation "and their families" is used:

> *Bride and Groom*
>
> *And their families*
>
> *Invite you to the wedding*

Traditions and customs have changed and the above wedding invitations reflect this. They are also statements of how a couple locates the celebration of their marriage in the emotional and social map of their families. They either allocate importance to family, emphasising the role of family and parents in this event, or, in contrast to that, they may emphasise the role of the couple itself as hosts who are in charge of this event. In this scenario parents and family are being allocated the role of guests, in line with friends who are, of course, not unimportant but by no means central.

Often this statement on the invitation may not mirror the financial reality of the wedding. Only in rare circumstances was the invitation issued by either the young couple alone or the parents alone matched by either of those parties actually financing the wedding exclusively. Given the economic reality of most weddings that I heard of, "X and Y and their families invite you" would be the most appropriate formulation.

Indeed the different formats of invitation were about more than finances: they rather seemed to be statements of intent as to who was in charge of this wedding, and this became particularly visible in the actual negotiations around who was going to be invited.

At all the weddings in this sample there was a mix of family and friends, most weddings having a rough balance of guests falling into two groups: there are on the one hand family, or friends of the parents who were known to the wedding couple and classed as near family. On the other hand, there are friends of the wedding couple. If there was an imbalance, then this was in most cases in this sample tipped towards more friends of the wedding couple, rather than of the parents, thus reversing tradition from even just a generation ago. Many mothers commented on this as a difference compared to their own weddings, although nobody objected to it as such. Mothers confessed to being at times disappointed that certain friends of theirs who may have been around during the childhood years of the bride or groom were not invited, but all of them were aware that budgets limited numbers of guests and that whoever was going to be invited should have some significance to the wedding couple and not just to the parents. What seemed to be experienced as more problematic in some cases was how the guest list was arrived at.

For some, this negotiation was a smooth process with the guest list developing as part of a conversation between all parties:

> Suzie (daughter) has felt that she is the hostess of this event and she is on the whole very relaxed about proceedings: "It [deciding on the guest list] wasn't that difficult. She said: 'who do you want to be there?' and I said whom I wanted and they are going to be there. We just sat down and talked about it."

> Beverly says that both she and her daughter wrote their own guest lists and "then we put them together".

> Sheila suggested a couple of their own friends to her daughter and "she just jumped at it and said, 'absolutely'."

Other mothers talked about not really knowing at all who was going to be invited and feeling that they were not at all involved in discussions and decisions around the guest list:

> Marie (daughter): "She did ask who we would want to be there, but we were definitely at the end of the queue... I didn't even know for ages how many members of our family we were allowed to invite. It was very clearly: 'we have to wait how many of our friends will accept and then if there are any spare places, you can squeeze some of your people in...' It wasn't that I wanted loads of family there; it was the feeling of being last in the queue, that's what hurts."

> Diane (son): "We weren't involved in the guest list at all. I said, 'it would be quite nice if a couple of friends could come who knew you as a child. He did not commit to that at all, only at the end, when some of his friends did not come, so there were a couple of slots left."

On the whole it is seen as a balancing act:

> Marion (daughter): "The invites, that has been a balancing act all the way through; it really was the difficult bit, the embarrassment of not being allowed to invite people who you know would expect to be invited... she just wanted all her young friends and there were people whose weddings we had attended, with her. It was a bit of a rift really."

Several mothers use the phrase "being allowed" to ask some people to come to the wedding who they would like to be there. This seemed to bear no correlation to how much they might contribute to the finances of the wedding. Only in one case where the understanding was clear that the parents paid for one part of the wedding (the reception and meal) and the couple paid for a different part (evening and disco), did the mother in question see this as an implicit agreement that she would be primarily in charge of the guest list for "her" part of the celebration. Whilst she was very happy to let her daughter have input and suggest which friends she wanted to be there, the mother did not feel she needed permission on whom to invite. Her daughter was in charge of the invitations for the evening part of the wedding. Another mother negotiates an extra table which she is going to pay for and which will be for friends of her and her husband:

> Marion sees herself as the hostess: "We are the official hosts, now that evolved, money may have come into it, they realised we contribute more than they thought", but negotiations are still not running smoothly: "My husband kept reminding me, 'we negotiated that table,' because, before you know it..."

In the majority of cases however mothers talk about having to ask permission to invite. The need to ask for permission to invite a guest to the wedding highlights the fact that the mother is most definitely not the hostess. The question again becomes, how special a guest is she? It is the place that she is allocated, in being mentioned or not mentioned on the invitation, or in being given a say in aspects of the guest list, that provides a commentary on where the mother's position is at this moment in time, as far as her role in her child's life is concerned. Moreover, it is experienced as predicting where she is going to be. Are her feelings and wishes important to her child? Can they be negotiated or will they be ignored? This may well be acted out as a power struggle, but underneath it the question is more one of loss and anxiety and how to deal with it. Reactions to invitations and guest lists are a prime example of what is so striking about weddings: what seems to be a case of severe overreaction turns out to make a lot more sense when looking at its emotional meaning.

If a map is drawn which locates the mother in a central or more removed position from her child, then there is also the question of how much room the other family are allocated. Most mothers were aware of an unwritten rule about a certain balance between the numbers of guests from both families. They commented on either their own family being rather large and outnumbering the other family, or feeling outnumbered by the other family. They felt often uncomfortable if the need for some sort of balance seemed not to be observed by their own child or the other family.

2.4 The other family

Invitations and guest lists do not just deal with the balance between family and friends, but also with the balance between the two families: this is after all a family event that involves at least two families, often families that may themselves already have been extended following parental split-ups and second marriages. If in the early interviews it was me who often had to bring the other family into the conversation, by now, in these second interviews, the families of bride and groom will have had more of an experience of each other.

All mothers are clear about the fact that this is, on one level, just about getting on with a new set of people that one has not chosen oneself. They compare it to meeting new neighbours, new colleagues or people one may meet when travelling on holiday. In all these circumstances our choice is limited and we have to make an effort to get on, even if we do not have that much in common. Some of the mothers felt lucky in that they did actually have something in common and got on with their child's new in-laws. Some confessed quite matter-of-factly that these would not have been people they would necessarily have chosen to spend time with, had it not been for their child's choice of partner, without necessarily seeing this as a big problem. There were also mothers who were quite open in their reservation about or even dislike of the other family.

What they all knew however was that the issue was not primarily their own relationship with this new set of people, but rather their child's relationship with them. Moreover, would this new relationship their child was forming, not just with their new partner, but with this new family, somehow threaten or at least change the relationship between themselves and their child? Would their bond be stretched and extended to incorporate a new family or would it take something away from the original bond?

It is in this context that the wedding preparations are experienced as a kind of "taster" of things to come.

One factor that had influenced this experience from the start seems to be the question of territorial advantage or disadvantage, in other words the location of the wedding in its proximity to either set of parents. By now decisions have been made about this:

Angie's son is getting married near her own home and she admits to feeling relaxed about the wedding partly because of the location: "I don't want to interfere and I don't need to."

What seems to make the difference is that mothers whose children chose a location at or near their parents see the choice of location near them as a statement about their child's continuing appreciation of "home" and family of origin:

Angie's son is getting married near his parents' home: "It feels wonderful that it is local... here where the children grew up. It feels very nice that W feels very connected to this part of the world, to his family."

Suzie's daughter is getting married in a ceremony in the garden of her childhood home and Suzie says: "I would have been sad had she wanted to get married from anywhere else; my stepson got married from his in-laws' house which was a very grand setting. And yet: I would have been sad. It would have been jealousy: she trusts somebody else more than me... It's about home, it's her saying 'here and nowhere else, it is still a significant place for me'... it is about her being able to say to everybody: 'this is my home.'"

In this context the choice of venue near "home" is read as a statement about the continuing link with the child's own family and an appreciation of its importance. At the very time when the son or daughter is not only marking the beginning of having his or her own family, but also joining another family (his or her family-in-law), this statement about the strength of the connection with the family of origin is hugely reassuring to these mothers. The change that this wedding symbolises is less threatening to them. The wedding on the territory of one's own family may add practical stress around the preparation, but it removes a big source of anxiety at a deeper level and eases the transition.

This deeper anxiety is noticeable in the mothers who do not have the territorial advantage. It emerges in their conversations when talking not just about the venue, but about their contact with the other in-law family and their involvement with the wedding. Mothers by this stage have got a fairly good idea which family is dominant in the wedding preparation and how this impacts on them:

Moira's daughter is getting married near her in-laws: "She has been scooped up by his family. I am delighted for her, but... [laughs] jealousy, yes there might be." Later she says about the wedding that takes place in the groom's local church: "It was their local church... the mother of the groom had clearly played a huge part in her daughter's wedding and was likely to play a huge role again... [laughs]... she sings in the choir, she knows the people who do the flowers... There were times... K [daughter] kept checking whether I was ok about it."

Fiona's son got married recently and she remembers the wedding preparations: "His mother-in-law was in charge. She said, 'it's for the bride, the wedding,' and I really felt for my son. It wouldn't have mattered what his identity was; for the wedding she saw him as "the groom" who was needed... 'As long as you marry our daughter and give us this day...' Her son just got engaged and apparently she said, 'oh, it's not the same, you want to get involved, but really, you know, you don't get a say.' And I thought, 'well, you realise that now.'"

Shirley is upset: "My daughter is getting married and his family are there."

A WEDDING IN THE FAMILY

Marion comments on her son taking a position in the background; all negotiations around the wedding are conducted by his bride-to-be: "She [daughter-in-law] asked for various things [for the wedding]... she is the one in charge."

Whilst here the words "in charge" seem to indicate a power struggle over control over the day, I think the deeper anxiety is rather about the family boundary being drawn around the in-law family and the wedding couple, with their "own" family being allocated a secondary role. It is not so much the wedding event that matters, but the future positioning of both families in their importance to the new couple. It is therefore not surprising that the territorial advantage of the other family becomes meaningless if the own family is seen as dominant in other respects:

Claire whose daughter is getting married in her new mother-in-law's church is very relaxed about this: "A lot of people have commented on this, but actually I think it balances things out a bit." She knows that the young couple will live closer to her than the other family and has stated earlier of her new son-in-law: "He likes the way we do things better than the way his own family do them; he is quite open about that."

The impact of all of this is hugely influenced by how contact between the two families, in particular the two mothers, unfolds during the preparations for the wedding. Communications about the mothers' wedding outfits are often used as a start to some kind of contact prior to the wedding, equally keeping each other informed about preparations. There are several mothers who are in regular text, phone or email contact with the "other" mother:

Suzie tells me of lots of texting with the other mother: "I text I've done this or that and she immediately texts back."

Angie (son): "We got to know the other parents quite well. Other mother and I are in secret contact about things, a little surprise for the day."

Barbara (son) tells of lots of email communication between herself and the other mother: "Dress, general chitchat." This other mother also insisted that, in spite of the wedding being held at her location, the invitations should be in joint names by both parents.

Sheila (daughter) has had good contact with her daughter's future parents-in-law: "We are lucky, we get on really well. We can envisage Christmases together, children's parties..." Before the wedding both sets of parents look at wedding venues together with the couple; the two mothers even go shopping for their wedding outfits together.

Jill's daughter is getting married abroad, so her own role in the wedding preparations is quite reduced. However, she stresses the other mother's empathy and reaching out: "She [the other mother-in-law] asked me: 'how do you feel about your daughter marrying a foreigner? Are you feeling sad that she is so far away?' And I thought, 'how considerate. She is a lovely person, they are interested in you, interested in people.'"

Monica (son) talks of emails: "What we are wearing, that sort of thing."

Helen, who really likes her son's future parents-in-law, actually goes shopping together with the bride, the bride's mother and sister, and her own other daughter-in-law who will be bridesmaid. The five women look together for a wedding dress for the bride and after that for their own outfits. "It was like an outing with friends. The shop assistant said she had never seen anything like it!"

If this type of contact and reaching out is missing or not reciprocated, it is experienced as very negative:

Jane's daughter is living near her in-laws. Jane is not impressed with the other family: "His mum invited us on one occasion which was nice and we met the family... but we were observers. They weren't really incorporating us, they weren't really interested in us. They are very insular, it's all about them."

Deborah, whose daughter is getting married near her new husband's family, is put off by the other mother's lack of response: "I tried to encourage a bit of contact with her [the mother of the groom], but she was not really interested and hardly responded: it took her weeks and weeks to answer emails, or she did not answer them at all. Quite rude really."

Equally, it can be the general lack of interest shown by the other family in the wedding that is the issue:

Michele (son) describes the other family as "too pre-occupied with their own lives. That over shadows the wedding."

Melanie, who struggles with her role as mother of the bride, reports that her daughter declares her future parents-in-law "difficult people". "She says they are not really that interested". Melanie sees the irony though in her daughter predicting that these parents will "just come along," "very much like she suggests I should do, actually".

Fiona says about her daughter's future mother-in-law: "Apparently she feels she has not done enough, but she never offered anything." There is no direct contact or communication between these two mothers.

Beverly (daughter) finds the other family "fine, but very reserved".

Sometimes it is just a difference between the families that is noted, and predictions of contact vary accordingly:

Gina (son): "There is a slight social difference, urban/rural, intellectual, possibly political...I wouldn't assume that we would get to know each other very much".

What most of these mothers seem to wish for is at least an acknowledgement by the other family that their child is important and welcomed into the new family and that to a degree they, the mothers, are too:

Melanie, who is struggling with her role as the mother of the bride, is delighted when she is told that the groom's grandmother "would really love to meet you" and by warm words is welcoming her daughter into the family.

Barbara talks about emails from her son's future mother-in-law: "She said, 'my friends are all delighted, he [son] is a lovely guy.' She keeps saying that about my son, which is nice."

Beverly talks with the mother of the groom who was married before: "So I said to her, 'are you ok about this? After all, you have been through this before.' And that was good, it was all out in the open. And she was nice: 'this is different, your daughter brings out the best in him.'"

There are noticeable undercurrents of competition and rivalry. Rivalry with the in-law family is often made light of in humorous remarks, but sometimes a more serious side shines through:

Angie is amused: "Her dad had begun to invite people. I believe he had to be reined in a bit."

A WEDDING IN THE FAMILY

Diane (daughter) brings in a bit of competition in a humorous way: "She [other mother] said she thought she might wear a hat and then we could have had a Hat Off."

Jeanne (daughter) seems to quite enjoy the following observation about the other family: "His [the groom's] mum is adding people to the list, saying 'this best friend and that best friend'. She is adding people to the list and L [daughter] is getting nervous," [laughs].

Marion talks about the other mother's outfit for the wedding: "She'll get something really nice, she'll top me."

Irene thinks her daughter's mother-in-law "wants to have a lovely wedding, because she did not have one herself," but also suspects that "she likes to organise family events, but everything has to happen at hers... they don't want a big wedding, if it is not their occasion." The future in-law family arranged an engagement party "without consulting me, without checking whether I was available; nobody else from my family was invited." Later she tells with some satisfaction that the other mother got short shrift when trying to influence who was going to be invited to what part of the wedding: "I never had any conflict about that with my daughter."

Michele (son) feels that the other family are spoiling things in not supporting her daughter-in-law sufficiently. She thinks the mother of the bride "wants it to be all about her, she wants to dress young ... When her [bride's] family came over, she dropped us and all of a sudden she was always around at her sister's and mum's, but not anymore."

Louise (son) comments on the other family: "I sensed a competitiveness. I come from a professional family; they come from a business background, not doing that well. I wondered whether he felt insecure in comparison."

The strongest indication of how deep this rivalry can run comes from a conversation I had informally with a colleague who was not one of my interviewees. Prior to her daughter's wedding, her future son-in-law's mother was diagnosed with a recurring cancer with a very poor outcome prognosis. My colleague confessed that her first reaction was one of near triumph that she was going to be the only grandmother to any future grandchildren. She said she was absolutely horrified by her own reaction: she liked and got on with the other mother and had not even be aware of any rivalry before this thought just came up, seemingly from nowhere!

I think it is in the context of this rivalry that we can locate a sense of pleasure when one's own child is perhaps not entirely happy with something that is part of the other family's culture:

> *Angie describes her future daughter-in-law as very organised and her mother as having clear opinions, whereas "my son and I are a bit more laid back".*

> *Barbara, who is finding the amount of money spent on the wedding by the bride's family quite difficult, is rather relieved at her son's discomfort about it: "He really thinks some of it is ridiculous. We don't talk about it a lot, as she is very much into it." "I liked the fact that he would go there with me."*

> *Fiona's daughter invited her mother and mother-in-law to her hen-do, but her mother-in-law declined. "We are resigned to it, it is what it is. If they don't want to, they don't want to", the "we" telling the story of a joint reaction in mother and daughter.*

> *Irene talks of her daughter "already trying not to do too much with her mother-in-law. Things are not going too well between them [the couple] and her [mother-in-law]."*

Louise says about her son and his future in-law family: "He is a bit more like us... He is fine with them, but I don't think they have in any way replaced us. I would not want him to run them down and he wouldn't. The only thing he ever said [about his future mother-in-law], she does not like silence [laughs]."

Here the child's alignment with the mother serves as a reassuring statement that the original family bond is not threatened by the newly formed bond with the other family. Equally important is to get some sort of reassurance about the bond of the new son-in-law or daughter-in-law with the mother's family:

Beverly described with pleasure how much their future son-in-law fits into their family: "He has fitted into this family, as if this is the one he was looking for. Like: 'I've found my people'."

Melanie recalls a meeting with her daughter's future parents-in-law prior to the wedding: "There were some interesting moments. We were talking a bit about their son whom we know quite well; he is very much part of our family. Suddenly his mother looked at me and said: 'you seem to know my son a lot better than I know your daughter.' I realised I knew a lot more about proceedings than she [other mother] does. She seemed a bit out of the loop. I felt a sadness for her." She also admits "There was a lot of relief after that meeting" and around the same time things seemed to lighten between her and her daughter: "I felt a lot less anxious and a lot less excluded. We started to laugh about things. We definitely turned a corner. We had silly laughs; we were in this together."

She does admit to feelings of pleasure when her daughter makes a slightly dismissive comment about her new mother-in-law. Melanie suggested for example: "'Isn't J's mum very much like her own mum?' And she [daughter] said, 'not really, Mum. She tries to, but she doesn't pull it off.' That absolutely cracked me up."

This last mother has had a rather hard time with the preparation and her daughter's comment clearly alleviated anxieties about how excluded or included she felt herself.

If the own family is seen as central and the couple are perceived as belonging more to one's own family than the other one, then generosity is possible:

> *Tricia is concerned about her daughter's mother-in-law: "I don't always agree with how little my daughter allows his mother to do [for the wedding]. She can only see it from her point of view. I can also see the mother's perspective. To me she feels left out a bit; to my daughter she feels overbearing."*

> *Jeanne is very happy and approving of her daughter's attempts to include her future mother-in-law in many aspects of the wedding: "It addresses the balance a bit. She has had ups and downs with her [mother-in-law], so I think this good, to really have her involved." Even her daughter's suggestion that the mother-in-law should join them when going shopping with her for her wedding dress is met with a relaxed response: "She said, 'how would you feel if we went together with X [mother-in-law] to look for a dress?' and I said, 'absolutely fine'."*

Are we talking about petty issues here? Are these mothers unnecessarily setting up a scenario that involves competition and jealousy? There was no doubt in the interviews that this was not just an issue for some women, but was present in nearly all of the interviews. After all this is precisely what a wedding brings into sharp focus: there are two families here with an equal "claim" to this wedding and, more importantly, to this couple, and both families have to adjust to that. This is bound to be a bit of a bumpy ride and anxieties about how this is going to turn out and how the own family will fare and come out the other side compared to the other family are not at all surprising.

Again and again the question is: where is the mother going to find herself in this redrawing of boundaries between her own family and the new family? Where are her child and their new husband/wife positioning themselves as the connecting link in the middle? Family boundaries are changing, attachments are renegotiated, loosened or strengthened: the wedding again makes all this visible.

2.5 Maternal tiptoeing continued and the generous and the not so generous child

If there is fear of losing one's child to the other family and being relegated to the role of the less important family, then there are certain factors that are helpful or unhelpful for these mothers to contain those fears and keep them in perspective. One crucial factor is the quality of interaction between the mother and her child as it has by now unfolded in the preparation of the wedding.

Most mothers comment on the fact that there seems to be a regressive quality in their relationship with their child at this time. This sometimes means a regression to a more playful, earlier stage of the mother/child relationship. In particular, mothers of brides tell of a nearly "Blue Peter"-ish kind of activity, preparing details of table decorations, looking at colour schemes, collecting jam jars:

As Marie puts it: "The glitter stuff".

Sheila: "Flowers, petal, confetti, bunting, you name it…"

Suzie: "I think about it a lot. I dreamt the other night about plastic buckets for flowers, where to get the cheapest… those sort of details… a lot of handmade stuff. We spent a weekend painting tin cans, I made confetti… I have made a lot of pompoms… I have discovered there are 'seconds' of petals" [laughs in mock confusion].

Fiona is on the phone to her daughter every day, discussing little details of the day: "We sort of go, 'what do you think of this? What do you think of that?' We have the same ideas about colours… it's not a chore, we like doing this sort of thing."

Alex (daughter) talks about the nice aspects of the wedding preparation: "Decorating the venue... M [daughter] and I from the onset have had fun thinking about that, slightly DIY, that's a style we both like. It's been very positive, we've both homed in on that, using Pinterest, sharing pictures and ideas."

However, the majority of women talk about a different kind of regression, often a regression to difficult teenage years. They describe the complicated task of trying to get it right in the face of possible tension and irritations:

Melanie is looking back on the months of wedding preparations: "Mostly it's great, it's organised, but mostly I have been surprised by people's reactions, most of all by my daughter who has been quite stressed by it all. I don't know how to describe it, grumpy, her sister says... Perhaps I've got to learn, an adult daughter with her own mind and I've seen myself as a bit of a pain in the neck, rather than 'mum will sort it out'. It's not just about now, but about old stuff! Am I doing too much or too little?"

In fact her uncertainty about what kind of help would be welcome to her daughter is very clear: "It's a difficult task for all of us how to read her... I don't know why I feel so tentative. I have my mother's engagement ring. She [daughter] never knew my mother; it would be a link with the past and I have been thinking, 'what if she doesn't want it?' I want to give her something, but I don't know whether it is welcome."

Angie, whose son is getting married near his childhood home which makes her very relaxed about other details, is cautious about offering any kind of opinions. When she sees the invitations which do not mention the parents at all, she thinks: "Oh, it's not usually done like this [couple inviting]. I noticed it, and then I thought..., but I didn't ask, 'perhaps different in Spain'." And on another occasion: "I just thought then, I did not say though, 'I don't want to be a nuisance.'"

Alex (daughter): "When we see them for lunch, we may be trying to bring it up, casually, you know, just wondering, just checking."

Even commenting on the wedding dress becomes a difficult task. Melanie (daughter): "I commented and it was ok, I bit the bullet and it was ok."

Beverly, who is very much seeing herself as the hostess of her daughter's wedding and had been invited by her daughter to be that, recalls: "She was getting cross, because I was going faster than she thought I needed to go... I don't know what it was, but she just exploded and I got very upset. I discovered afterwards that there were problems at work and I learned to be a bit more mindful about how to approach things."

Barbara says about her future daughter-in-law: "I don't know her that well, I have been cautious, cautious about offering opinions."

Helen is enjoying the wedding preparations, but even she emphasises the need for caution: "We would like to give them a surprise present, the music in church, but of course you have to be careful. When they talk about their plans, I may ask a question, when I think they may have overlooked something. You have to be careful, of course."

Sometimes the tiptoeing is actually not so much based on the anxiety not to be overbearing, but rather the opposite: here the question becomes, "Am I giving enough?"

Tricia says she is only involved with details of the wedding when her daughter needs her "hiring and firing mainly". She is worrying: "I am sometimes wondering whether I am doing enough, not sure she would ask, but then there is only so many times you can say: 'do you want any help?' I think it's ok, she knows what she wants."

In the middle of all this uncertainty and caution the concept of generosity makes an appearance again, as something that can make all the difference to the mother's experience: daughters-in-law keeping the other family involved, the young couple openly keeping parents informed, showing them brochures, early plans etc:

Angie (son): "M [daughter-in-law] has been very generous to me by including me in the thinking about the wedding. I've been to two wedding fairs and she invited me to the first dress fitting with her parents and her grandma."

Louise (son): "They talked over all their plans with us... she showed us the invitations. I was invited to and went with her to look at a wedding dress. I was invited to that from the beginning, very nicely."

Michele (son): "M [daughter-in-law] has tried to get me quite involved, she keeps inviting me to things." She has been asked to be her daughter-in-law's maid of honour: "I feel very honoured that she asked me."

Barbara, who had not had the chance to get to know her future daughter-in-law that well and who is going to travel to another country for the wedding where the other family and the young couple live, is pleased to be offered plenty of opportunity to talk with her about it: "H [daughter-in-law] has been continuously checking things out with us. They have been really good about that. It's been nice to talk with her about it. M [son] is a bit fed up with it by now."

In contrast to that:

Diane feels very excluded from the preparations for her son's wedding: "She [daughter-in-law] has never really allowed us a relationship... She has never wanted to talk about girlie stuff... [laughs], and there is a wedding which involves girlie stuff. I have not been invited to do anything to do with the wedding."

Fiona is equally upset about being excluded: "We have no say in it at all. I asked to see the template for the invitations [for which they said they would pay] and she [daughter-in-law] came round and said, 'these are the ones we have ordered. If you don't like them, we'll pay for them ourselves."

Maggie's son is getting married in a venue local to her home, but she is not asked to be involved in any of the preparations, which are handled by the bride's family: "I feel a bit used... We weren't told anything about what was going to happen on the day. She had an itinerary, timed to perfection, but we only found out about it through our other son who was best man."

The above quotes are from mothers of sons who were aware of their slightly more marginal role in the wedding preparations and therefore were particularly appreciative if future daughters-in-law were inviting them in.

The presence or absence of generosity is especially commented on by mothers of daughters. If across tradition the groom's family is the dominant family and has the "territorial advantage", these mothers search for a role not just for the day, but also for the time of preparing and managing the wedding preparations. This group could be seen to be struggling right from the start in the early interviews. "Generosity" is commented on by mothers in this group as an attitude that can be shown or withheld on the part of their own child and the "other family". If there is at least an acknowledgement that this cross-tradition situation is a difficult one and the mother's feelings are at least validated by the own child, by their partner or by the other family, then the adjustment to this situation is easier:

> Moira's daughter is getting married in the local church near her future parents-in-law. Does she feel jealous? "Jealousy? Yes, there could be that... but my daughter is very aware of that and they are making a real effort to spend time with us... She makes a point of making contact without the other family necessarily being involved. She is just very careful to keep me involved. I was invited to the hen-do: that was lovely." Later: "His mother is also sensitive to our situation which makes a big difference."

Contrast this with experience of Marie whose daughter also gets married near her husband's parents:

> Marie: "She [her daughter] just pretended this was perfectly normal and a non-issue and did not acknowledge <u>once</u> that we may feel upset, or indeed that she appreciated that we did not make an issue out of it."

> Shirley's daughter is getting married near her future in-law family: "I am not involved in anything; they are leaving me out of the equation altogether. I am getting fairly upset I suppose."

> The same goes for Jane (daughter): "I have to be so careful, particularly because she has struck up such a strong relationship with his mother. You can write yourself out of the script, so I just have to be careful."

Even in relatively straightforward scenarios with mothers of brides preparing the wedding together with their daughters, there is a sense of relief and appreciation if the daughter is "generous":

Suzie: "she gave me a role and I am grateful."

What this indicates is that in nearly all scenarios the mothers feel that the power is located with their child, the power to include or exclude the mother, the power to consider the mother's feelings or not, the power to make her feel part of this wedding.

This is interesting in that again the question "who owns this wedding?" is emotionally quite separate from finances. As far as most of the mothers are concerned, it is their child who owns this wedding. Again, most of them think that this is how it should be; in fact they may have painful memories of their own weddings where the opposite was the case and they were getting married with their parents being in charge:

> *Michele (son) speaks for many of them: "It's their right to have the wedding they want."*

What most mothers did not seem to be prepared for was how they may feel as a result of it. It is not a question any more of who owns this wedding, nor a question of who is in charge of this wedding, but rather, "How important am I for this wedding and how much am I included in the preparation of it?" All of a sudden, they may be dependent on their child's "goodwill" and indeed generosity. This is where old fault lines may well break open, exposing difficulties in the relationship with this particular child. Many mothers cannot help but comment that all this may be different with a different child:

> *Melanie, who is highly aware of the sibling rivalry between her two daughters, and this showing in the wedding preparations: "It's quite primitive stuff... and it got worse, probably compounded, I think ... looking at her sister, and I think, 'it won't be like that [with her]'."*

This means that mothers who are not shown generosity are not just struggling with their feelings about the wedding, but they face some potentially quite disturbing feelings about the kind of person they observe their child to be and the kind of relationship they have with them:

Marie, who had complained about the lack of consideration in her daughter, wonders: "How can she be so self-centred? How can she care so little about how I feel, when I try so hard to consider how she feels? It is scary when you look at your own child and you think: 'I don't really like you very much, [pauses], when you are like this.' And you begin to think, 'maybe that is the person she is, or maybe just with me?'"

Another mother, Lauren, whose daughter can be quite "bristly", associates this with earlier years during her daughter's teens. She, like many other mothers, is aware of the regressive quality of her exchanges with her daughter: "I made a couple of suggestions, little stuff, you know, just ideas to play around with, and she just nearly bit my head off. It's like we are back there, when for quite a while we had been much more like two adults, well, not any more since this wedding business." She also however wonders how truly "adult" the previous years had been: "Maybe we are just grown up with each other when there is no pressure... maybe when there is pressure, it'll always be like this."

Marion says about her daughter who she feels has excluded her from most of the wedding preparations: "She is not aware of how I feel, but she is very neglectful and I have to admit I am very disappointed. When my stepson got married, there were flowers for all three mothers. They were really sensitive to my feelings. Nothing like that is coming from my own daughter."

The opposite can be seen in mothers with children who are relating in a more open and generous way with their mothers around the preparations:

> *Suzie, who is describing the wedding preparations as a cooperative endeavour between herself and her daughter: "we just sat down and talked about it. Some of the ideas are mine; we send each other stuff. She knows immediately... she is not bridezilla like, she just knows what she wants, but she is happy for me to make suggestions." As a result she does not just find the wedding preparations easy, but is looking at her daughter in renewed appreciation: "she is so lovely, she is such a lovely girl, she is so strong and bright too."*

What the wedding preparation seemed to do was to force mothers to look at the quality of their relationship with their child prior to the wedding. Whatever emerged here was often felt not to be entirely new: the generous or not so generous child, the excluding or including child, did not emerge just as a result of the wedding, but old fault lines often broke open and could not be ignored any more.

Of course, for me as the interviewer, it is intriguing to speculate on what the sons and daughters of these women might have to say. Would the generous ones talk of generous and easy mothers and the difficult sons and daughters of pushy and difficult mothers? I have no way of telling. A question of chickens and eggs, or rather mother hens and quite grown-up chickens, to stay with a well-known phrase. What I could see however was that all of these mothers were aware of the danger of interfering and, on the whole, approved of their child being in charge of this wedding. I could also see that there was a noticeably regressive quality to some of the feelings and encounters and that a lot of the mothers found the regressive move back to more conflict-driven stages of the mother/child relationship very difficult. A lot of them were certainly taken by surprise by this regression.

2.6 Memories of "easier love"

In the middle of all this regression and tiptoeing, other memories emerge of times when being a mother was perhaps easier:

Melanie, whose daughter is getting married, shows me a photo of her son and grandson, trying on their identical suits for the wedding. She confesses: "My heart melted when I saw it, they are so close, so alike, such easy happiness on their faces."

It is only when we explored why this photo had such a powerful effect on her, that it becomes clearer: what you see on the photo is a parent and a child who are perfectly at ease with each other, the little boy still being so proud to look just like his dad: quite the opposite of the current state of affairs between Melanie and her daughter, where separation and conflict rule the day. The photo is a reminder of days gone by, and a painful reminder at that.

Barbara dreams of her son as a child: "It's quite strange I had a dream about M the other day, about him as a boy of seven or eight… I felt very emotional, I cried when I woke up… this connection with that little boy, just that feeling, how much I knew him then, and I don't anymore. I have been carrying that around with me." This leads to feelings around being aware of his vulnerability on the day but not being the one who can help him. Somebody else is now there for him: "That realisation has been growing."

Angie says: "I am thinking back quite a lot, my mother's wedding, my own, my son's childhood."

What is noticeable is that whilst a wedding is a ceremony that celebrates a new union, a step into the future for the wedding couple and their families, it also means for most mothers a looking back into the past:

> Melanie: "It is not just about now, but about old stuff." She has looked at old family albums: "weddings, children, funerals, life cycles".

> Sheila (daughter) also looks at old photos: "You know, just looking at the memories."

> Emily who has been asked to provide old family photos for her daughter's wedding tells of being quite tearful when she looks at these pictures: "It was so easy then; when she needed something she would ask for me and it was all so easy and straightforward. That love was just so straightforward. Helping her was just so straightforward."

Again, it is noticeable that, whilst for the child the wedding is all about the future, for the mother it is also about the past and her relationship with her child over the years.

2.7 THE dress

As the previous chapter describes, memories of earlier times emerge. In fact, they do not just emerge as direct recollections, as sudden images long forgotten, or in dreams, but the mother/child interaction seems at times to have a quality that makes it feel like a kind of re-enactment in the here and now.

I think one of those re-enactments can be observed in the rituals and feelings around the purchase of the bride's dress, and later in the "getting the bride ready" on the day.

For mothers of brides the choosing of the wedding dress is without exception a crucial part of the wedding preparations. Culturally, the importance of the dress is huge. The bridal dress is nearly universally the centrepiece of a wedding event. In most cultures the bridal dress and the secrecy surrounding it are important. In some cultures the bride will change several times during the day and there is always a part of the wedding celebration that involves female members of the family getting the bride ready.

The white dress of the Western wedding has an iconic quality and various rituals are associated with it. It is for example kept secret from the groom, and often from nearly everybody else apart from a few close women. The mother of the bride always knows, in some cases also the mother of the groom, with good luck being attributed to keeping to the dress a secret. Whilst I was shown some photos of wedding dresses before the weddings, this was without exception done with a certain hesitation, wondering whether it would be all right to do so.

Who is included in the search for the dress in Western weddings holds significance and is being managed with great care. Even mothers of brides who were hardly involved in other aspects of the wedding preparations were at some stage involved in the searching for and choosing of the dress, and often remember it as a significant and emotional occasion. This seems to be the case even for mothers who might find the whole idea of the bride in white, the financial and ideological implications, complicated or even objectionable. I came across only one mother who reported her daughter's father being present at the choosing of the dress. There were some mothers of grooms who were invited to look at the bride's dress at an early fitting and they were aware that they had been offered something "generous" and appreciated the invitation:

> Helen (son): "I had not expected that at all; that was something really special and I felt enormously happy about it."

Only one mother of a groom who had been invited to her daughter-in-law's dress fitting had declined, as she found the whole emphasis on the dress rather objectionable:

> Viv (son): "I said [to daughter-in-law] 'I'm sure you'll choose something nice, but it's not really my thing.' When my own daughter heard about it, she was really shocked that I had said that."

Viv's daughter, sister of the groom, "knew" that her mother had declined an important honour, the sharing of an intimate moment that often is reserved to bride and mother of the bride, and she told her mother off in no uncertain terms.

Why is it so important? Certainly for mothers of daughters it may offer an opportunity to capture something of the easy love of early days. Mothers of sons and daughters will have dressed and undressed their children, they will have bought their clothes, washed them, repaired them. Mothers of girls in particular are likely to have memories of their little girls' nearly inevitable princess phase, if that is the little girl she was, involving dressing-up boxes, party dresses, getting them ready for occasions, doing their hair. Clothes will have marked time: school uniforms, prom dresses perhaps, first interview and work outfits. They may have swapped clothes, or argued about them, but, either way, the task of looking at their daughter and saying "you look lovely", hoping to make her feel good about herself: all that will go back a long way. Inevitably the mother's opinion on her daughter's choice of clothes may have become less sought after, or mothers may or may not find it so easy any more to say and feel "you look lovely", but here they are asked again to do that very thing. The bride knows that there is no hiding on the day: she will be looked at by everybody and she is supposed to look beautiful. It takes a very confident young woman to not be at least a little anxious about this. It is in this situation that she may seek the maternal gaze as confirmation once more and mothers know that and respond to it. It does not work like that for all mothers; however, most mothers are aware that they are somehow supposed to feel something special and may be anxious that they are failing the test if they don't:

Beverly recalls that she felt her daughter "wanted me to be all emotional about the dress... she said 'I hope you cry when you see me in this dress.' But it just does not press my buttons."

Fiona describes the scene of the wedding dress purchase: "It's supposed to be emotional, but it wasn't. I didn't cry; I wondered whether my daughter was disappointed..." [laughs].

Marion is clearly less happy with the dress than she feels she is supposed to be: "She looked lovely, but... I suppose she is big, but she looked nice. I would have preferred it a bit more... longer sleeves, but out of those she tried on... She looked lovely, but I wouldn't call it perfect."

For most mothers however, something special seemed to happen on that occasion: here they are sure that they are important once more and appreciated, and this can lead to close moments:

Melanie: "The dress, that was very important, that was the one thing, really, really important. And then something wonderful happened, she said, 'Mum, can we look at one, just the two of us?' That was a lovely moment."

Barbara was determined to pay for her daughter's dress: "I was just saying to C [future son-in-law], 'ok, you can take over now, but this is the last thing I can do for my daughter.'"

Sheila, who is not allowed to play a big part in her daughter's wedding preparations: "At least I wanted to give her the veil as a present." She was worried that her daughter who is struggling with her weight might not find the right dress: "I was so worried we would not find anything, so in the end I was very emotional, because she did look so lovely."

Marie, who felt quite excluded from most of the wedding preparations, recalls looking for the dress with pleasure: "We both knew when she found the right one, it was just right for her, and we both felt quite excited and enjoying it together, and we went for lunch afterwards and talked about the wedding the way I had expected we would talk about it, it was fun for the first time."

Helen was there together with the bride's mother when her future daughter-in-law tried on her wedding dress for the first time: "It was really moving. When she turned round, she looked nearly luminous, we all had tears in our eyes."

Alex remembers looking at dresses together with her daughter: "There was a warmth between us, it's a way of building a relationship, yeah, and it is really important to her."

Deborah remembers her daughter ringing her at work: "It was about the dress: she had been really happy with it, and then at the fitting, *she had put on some weight, and she felt it made her look fat. Her friend was with her and reassured her, but she was still very upset. I was in the middle of a meeting, it really was a bit tricky really, but I was, well, upset for her, but actually, yes, I suppose I was really happy: that she wanted me at that moment, she wanted Mum."*

Tricia is very emotional thinking of seeing her daughter in the wedding dress for the first time: "It was amazing, I didn't think I was going to cry, but I did. I am waiting for her to show me, and I am thinking, 'Oh my God, am I not going to be moved by this? Am I not being the mum who cries?' but when she came out and said, 'Mum, this is the one,' I cried." Trying to explain what was so moving, she says her daughter looked happy, but then adds, "it was seeing her look at me, 'what do you think, you need to think it is right as well', this expectant look."

It is these last two mothers who put their finger on this very important point: for mothers of daughters it is not really about the dress, it is about the reality of the daughter's expectant look, her "wanting Mum", and Mum's opinion and approval once more, that is the core of this early wedding dress experience. Mothers of daughters have a clear role here and it allows them moments of being involved and needed again: a chance to re-live something about their past relationship with their child, but also a statement about the present relationship, thereby reassuring them about the future.

Mothers of sons do not have that opportunity, but even they like being involved in buying or choosing their son's wedding outfit or parts of it. Some mothers bought the suit and helped choose it, one mother bought cufflinks, but I could not detect anything approaching a similar emotional charge as there was with mothers of brides.

For both mothers of sons and daughters alike, the other dress that matters is their own!

Everybody will look at the bride, but inevitably the mother of the bride and mother of the groom will also be scrutinised. Bridal shops often have a section for mothers; mother of the bride outfits can be found as a separate category in fashion departments, no doubt responding both to women's anxiety to get it right for this role and their corresponding preparedness to spend money! Several women commented on how these formal outfits felt alien to how they would normally dress, but they seemed to be unsure whether they could just follow their normal choice. Most of them sought their child's approval, not always getting it right first time round. They feel that it is important that their son or daughter approve of their choice and are not embarrassed or compromised by them:

Angie (son): "My son didn't like it; there was a lot of ivory in it. He thought it looked too much like a wedding dress [laughs]. Maybe I was a bit silly there."

Deborah (daughter): "Both my daughters said, 'Mum, that looks nice, but this is a wedding. Maybe you can find something a bit more, you know... [laughs]."

Irene (daughter): "What I mustn't be is ridiculous!"

Some mothers are even shopping together with their sons or daughters, but that is rare. It is quite clear that few of them feel that their child appreciates the mother's anxiety and need to be reassured. In some cases the scene in the wedding dress shop when mother provides the approving and emotionally charged feedback for her daughter, is mirrored when mother shows her own dress to her child:

Tricia (daughter): "I showed her the outfit when I had everything together. It was different from what she had expected and she said, 'oh my God, Mum, that looks perfect!'"

In most cases however, the essential "you look lovely" message, certainly needed by the brides, is also needed by the mothers and is sought from others: husbands and in most cases female friends or strangers. Several women showed me photos of their outfits and in some cases the dress itself; several of them were carrying pieces of material with them to find matching accessories, asking me sometimes directly what I thought:

> *Melanie tells about buying her dress on her own and proceeds to show me a photo: what do I think? She tells me of the scene in the clothes shop: "The thing that did it for me, I think it has to do with not really feeling part of this: I stepped out of the fitting room and an assistant turned round and said "Wow, that looks lovely."*

Here a stranger provides the message for Melanie that she had provided for her daughter, but nobody as yet had provided for her.

If the mother has found the right dress, the relief is enormous:

> *Sheila (daughter): "It was very important to look right. I bought it ages before the wedding; my daughter thought that was hilarious."*

> *Barbara expresses great relief at having found the right dress: "I want to show myself off and it is elegant, but relaxed, just right."*

> *Helen (son) is happy with her outfit, because it reflects what she wants to be on the day: "Elegant, but not in the foreground."*

The dress symbolises settling into a role at this day, an anticipation that things may be all right after all.

2.8 "I've got a life too"

Wedding preparations seem to go on for a long time these days. In most interviews the time between engagement and wedding was at least a year, in some cases around eighteen months. Of course there are phases of non-activity or low-level activity and phases of high activity and things tend to heat up towards the end. All in all, the event is on these mothers' minds for quite a lengthy period of time, even if there is nothing much to do for parts of it.

With all this prolonged focus on an event and its implication and the relational fallout of it, it is perhaps not surprising that with some mothers there is also eventually a bit of a shift in focus away from their child towards their own life.

Sometimes it is directly linked with the wedding: a number of mothers made holiday plans for after the wedding, sometimes making the most of the opportunities that a wedding abroad can give:

> Monica is planning a holiday after the wedding: "our own road trip... yeah!"

For some mothers the wedding is linked with other changes in their own lives which are independent from their child's life:

> Angie is retiring around the time of her son's wedding: "I had been thinking about it for a long time and the wedding suddenly seemed to change it. It seemed a good time to do it. It is connected: it is time for a change for me as well." She also puzzles about why she has recently rather dragged her feet responding to a request to give her menu choice for the wedding, and why the request, though she thinks it perfectly reasonable, has irritated her: "This wedding is all-consuming and we are thinking, there are other things in our life," and she adds: "I am also making changes, it is not just you."

Suzie has found her daughter's choice to get married from the family home very emotional and reaffirming. This is seen by her as her daughter's statement about the importance of her link to home. However, the other reason why it is important is that Suzie knows that this house will be sold soon, marking a transition for herself and her husband, moving themselves forward into a different phase of their lives. She does not want to be in a house waiting for daughters and grandchildren to visit her, but to live in a place that fits her and her husband's life as a couple: "That is our transition, nothing to do with her."

Gina confides that she has recently become secretly involved with another man.

Alex (daughter) is aware of major changes in her husband's and her own working life which need to be considered: "There is so much else going on in our lives. We haven't got time to worry about it all too much."

In this context it is often the case that mothers are not just in touch with their own pasts as mothers of their now grown-up child, but also with their own pasts *before* they had children, as young adults themselves. They may remember a more carefree self, more playful, and less weighed down by responsibilities. The mother who had an affair I think may fall into this category. Another mother tells with clear signs of enjoyment of a recent party:

Helen is amused about her own performance recently at a fancy dress party in a dress with a petticoat: "Never mind the wedding and the princess dress: we were dressing up as tarts and it was such fun."

There is a note of playful rebellion in this and similar statements, and as the interviewer I am invited to share this slightly guilty and pleasurable secret. The wedding symbolises a move away from the central role the mothers once played in their children's lives, and, as we have seen, this is often associated with anxiety and confusion. However, all these experiences – retirement, road trips, new projects or just fancy dress parties – indicate that the women are involved in a rebalancing act: the mother is not at the centre of her child's life any more, but the child, and with it the child's wedding, is not the overbearing centre of the mother's life any more either. Mothers experience loss, but some of them also taste a new freedom. The wedding yet again stands at the centre of this transition. As a true rite of passage for the whole family it is a marker of change and new balance, not just for the wedding couple, but also for the whole family and the mother in particular.

Chapter 3

The Big Day

Whilst I was in the process of working on this book I overheard by chance a conversation between two women on a train, one asking the other how the wedding day of her daughter had gone. The mother in question said that the day had actually been lovely. The other woman replied: "Well, in the end they all are."

This struck me at first as a bit of a dismissive remark, and yet when I went into the third round of interviews, I got more of a sense of what this woman may have meant. Indeed, with few exceptions, the mothers declared themselves pleased with the actual wedding day. In fact, particularly in the interviews that followed the weddings relatively quickly, one to two months afterwards, there was a palpable sense of relief and at times elation even. Most mothers declared themselves delighted with the day and clearly enjoyed enormously going through it in detail with me. However easy or difficult the preparations had been, the day itself tended to create heightened positive feelings: it was described as "lovely", "amazing", "wonderful", "fantastic", "better than I ever thought it could be".

Many mothers cried in the interviews recalling the day, a lot of them confessed to feeling strangely anti-climactic afterwards and often talked of a deep exhaustion following the state of feeling high after the day. The positive evaluation of the day sometimes seemed in contrast to some of the details of the day, such as, for example, tensions between the two families. However, the further away from the actual day the interviews were, the less these kinds of highly charged emotions were present, and, particularly in the retrospective interviews where mothers took me through the entire process in one single interview, there was no elation of this kind noticeable. The closer the mothers still were to the anticipation and tensions of the build-up to the day, the more intensely they seemed to feel the relief of having gotten through it and done so well.

My interviewees brought me photos, videos, speeches. I had asked whether they would be happy to bring any materials like that, but was quite struck by how much the mothers seemed to *want* me to see them. Some even attached photos of the wedding to their email replies to my invitation for a final third interview. There was no doubt at all: they enjoyed reliving the day and sharing this memory.

I found myself caught up in some of the anticipation and excitement, knowing when some of the weddings were going to be, being aware whether the weather was being kind, wondering how certain aspects of these weddings had gone, rooting for "my" mothers. The final build-up to the big day had its effect on everybody, including me, and I needed to step back in my mind before the interviews:

Angie (son): *"There is a sparkle effect. I knew this is unique, this won't happen again. I was aware of that and wanted to capture it. It seemed to go so quickly, it is really hard to hold on to it."*

Michele (son): *"I was in a bit of a fantasy land."*

Suzie (daughter): *"It was fantastic. It was just amazing, better than I ever hoped it would be. Somebody said, 'what would you change?' Not anything!"*

Irene (daughter): *"All went fantastically well, really fantastic."*

A WEDDING IN THE FAMILY

Melanie (daughter): "It was an amazing day. It exceeded everything I could have expected. I look back, all the anxiety, all the conflicts, all the tensions, how did it all melt away? It was quite extreme."

Indeed, this is the question, how did it all melt away?

The day as it unfolded followed, for most of them, a similar pattern: wherever the wedding took place, there were often preparations going on in the last days leading up to the wedding day, often involving both families. In most cases there was some kind of gathering the night before, with guests starting to arrive, whereas on the day itself the two families tended to withdraw into the smaller family of origin, with particularly the mother of the bride being busy getting her daughter "ready", until the actual wedding ceremony. The ceremony may be religious in nature or secular, it may not have even happened on the same day as the rest of the celebrations. Either way, it was then nearly always followed by some kind of reception, a sit-down meal with a seating plan, often some evening party with music and dancing. At some weddings not all the guests attended all parts of the day and often friends of the couple arrived for the later part of the party.

All weddings involved speeches; most had professional photographers, though sometimes a guest would perform that task. Whether the ceremony itself was of a religious nature or not, there would be an exchange of vows witnessed by family and friends. Most weddings saw the father of the bride walking his daughter towards the place of the ceremony, though there were some variations on this theme. All brides wore a white wedding dress or a dress that was special for the ritual of the wedding in their respective cultures. With secular weddings the ceremony often took place in the same location as the celebration; this may have been a specifically wedding-licensed hotel or venue, with barns being particularly popular, but there were also teepees and gardens in the bride's or groom's parents' home. If there was a registry office ceremony, this was often followed by a more festive ceremony, in some cases with nearly a year's delay, but more often soon after. Church weddings were followed by receptions at separate venues. There were winter wonderland weddings with fake snow, and mock and real country weddings, a rather more "urban" art deco wedding, but all of them had a hidden or more visible theme. Quite a lot of the mothers had described their child's wedding as "a bit different", "not formal", "a bit quirky", "they wanted it to be very much their own thing", the wedding with its variations around the ceremony and format being seen as another expression of the particular couple's individuality. However, it was clear that there was an underlying script of what a proper wedding consisted of and decisions to follow the "proper" format or deviate from it seemed to be made quite deliberately.

The role that the mothers of the bride and groom played on the day also varied a great deal. Most fathers of brides played their part in walking their daughter down the aisle and most of them gave a father of the bride speech, whilst most fathers of the groom had no immediately visible role on the day at all. The part of mothers varied hugely from woman to woman and wedding to wedding. All mothers of brides were involved in the getting ready of the bride on the morning of the day, but apart from that things were not that clear. Again, it became apparent in my interviews that there were underlying roles and expectations that had a bearing on how these women experienced the day. The underlying script of the "proper" wedding was something that all the mothers I interviewed were aware of. In either following it or rejecting it, or indeed feeling that they were not allowed to follow it, it informed how they behaved on the day and how they experienced the day. However the day turned out in the end, the preparation work that had been done in the lead-up formed part of the experience, and this undoubtedly included the emotional preparation work and the processing of the meaning of this big rite of passage for their families.

3.1 Hostess or special guest revisited

So what did mothers do on the day? Which role did they occupy in the end as hostess or special guest? This question after all had preoccupied the women I spoke to in the build-up to the wedding.

A few, as they had predicted and had maintained all the way through, were indeed hosting their child's wedding. Whatever work went on in the months before the wedding, things get extremely busy for these women who are hosting the wedding:

Suzie's daughter is getting married from the family home. The young couple, the other family, various friends, start arriving in the week leading up to the wedding. Everybody has come to help. She describes how "everything started happening, running on a serious amount of adrenalin... constantly looking at weather forecasts, gardening, making things, washing down tables, decorating things... people arriving, everybody just milling around, helping, bringing flowers, painting cans..."

Beverly is very much the hostess of her daughter's wedding. She too recalls the last weeks and days before the wedding as one big blur of preparations: "They had many last minute things to do. It was great, I was just buzzing all the time, things kept hitting me in the middle of the night. To be honest, I had got used to moving around at the pace of an old lady, so it was really lovely to rev it all up and be so quick."

Melanie's daughter is getting married in a venue near her mother's house. Many things are laid on by the venue, and yet there is plenty still to do for Melanie: "Sometimes I nearly felt I did not have enough to do, but I made back-up plans for everything, picking up dress, checking flowers all that."

On the day itself the hostess mother not surprisingly keeps buzzing:

> Suzie has been working hard all week: "Everything was done, we were ready! By the time it is all going on, there is an audience. Will everybody be ok? Will the sound system work? Has everybody got a drink? All of that begins to take over, the responsibility of being a hostess. This is how it is, we have to make sure that all these people are ok. I felt slightly sick all day, I could hardly eat anything, pure adrenalin, even during the best man's speech, I suddenly thought, 'did I put the lasagne in the oven for the band?' It just was full-on hostessing... There was this sense I could ruin something, it would be all my fault, but also I could give her something beautiful."

> Aysha is hosting her son's wedding in her house: "It's in my house, it is a party for my son... I want everybody to be ok, everybody to be happy. I never sit down, always on the go, I just want the day to finish and everything to be ok," and she adds in a rather powerful image: "I am like a sponge. I am trying to absorb everything, then slowly release."

> Beverly's anxiety is very much focused on the guests rather than the young couple: "I had to do the thinking about everything, or it might not happen."

> Nasreen feels the burden of being the hostess: "you are sitting there, looking at your family: are they happy? You are looking at the other family: are they happy? You are looking at your daughter: is she happy? I am not eating anything, I am eating all this information."

> Alex can hardly remember details as the last hours of preparations were frantic: "We had a frantic hour in the tent [last decorations] . It's all a bit of a blur... I think he [husband] did... no, I went... it's awful, did he drop me off there?"

Most mothers who were *not* the official hostess had spoken in the previous interviews about their confusion as to what exactly their role would be on the day. Many of them however seem to adopt a hostess role of sorts on the day, even if this has not been part of the official plan and set-up. However, a certain amount of confusion may remain:

Marion had paid for most of the wedding and had felt that gradually they had become the hosts, even if that had not been the way things had started off: "We went round to greet as many people as we could, we felt we had to mingle, we were the hosts." *Later she admits to some confusion about the host role. There was some problem with the meal provided by the hotel.* "We weren't quite sure whether it was up to us to complain, who it was up to actually."

Tricia (daughter) describes it as "some sort of balancing act on the day, just making sure that everybody is comfortable".

Diane had felt quite unhappy in the time leading up to the wedding. This wedding seemed to be dominated by the family of the bride, and Diane felt largely excluded: "I did not have a role on the day, [laughs]. We did not know anything about what was going to happen on the day until we got there. She [daughter-in-law] had an itinerary, timed to perfection. But it was our other son who was best man who sent it to us... I was determined on the day: I went round all the tables, I made sure they knew who I was. I just gave myself a bit of a role, I didn't miss a trick."

Moira had described how potentially difficult her daughter's wedding near the in-law family was, as she was not at all sure what her role on the day would be: "I did the hostessing on the day, introducing people to each other. My daughter also asked me to choose some music. I chose one piece I like... most of the music was done by his family, but this piece was performed by my nephew."

Michele's son is getting married at a neutral venue, but Michele knows more of the guests as the other mother lives abroad: "I was walking around and talking to different people, all of them really."

Irene describes how both sets of parents and the wedding couple greet the guests coming into the barn where the reception is being held.

Alex does not call herself the hostess, but is aware of certainly being a lot more than a guest: "It was all planned, it was busy, I was trying to look like a swan, whilst frantically paddling. I wasn't the hostess [laughs], I was the driver!" Later she says, "You are not in charge and you are not in control, but you feel responsible."

Eventually it may be possible to step back from the role of hostess: Melanie: "I eventually let go of something. At first, on the day, I was trying to do the right thing: I must go round and speak to everybody. I gave up on that in the end. There was no 'we never spoke to x'. I eventually stopped thinking I was responsible."

Mothers who do not find a hostess role at all for themselves on the day often find a different solution: they host a separate event. In some cases this separate event happens on their territory at a different time. One groom's family host a big engagement party. Other mothers host a separate wedding party after the main wedding if, for example, the wedding has taken place abroad and not all the family or friends could attend. Most of them however chose to host something separate for "their" guests, family and friends, maybe on the evening before the wedding. A lot of them focus their anxiety on the logistics of people getting to the wedding, whether "their" guests will make it in time:

Angie remembers how anxious she was that her guests would make it in time: "I developed an irrational anxiety about how long it would take people to get to the venue, being late. I rang people: 'remember the traffic'."

Tricia (daughter) is also anxious about the logistics and still worries at the wedding venue: "I just kept thinking, 'will everybody be there on time?'"

Alex, who had jokingly described herself as "not hostess, but driver" and had spent a lot of time working out the logistics of everybody and everything arriving at the right place at the right time, admits: "I had to have a map, to know where everybody was. I really did draw a map, so we would not lose people. I had to clear it in my own head."

These mothers also often invest time and sometimes money in finding appropriate accommodation for their family and friends which for some of them involves quite a lot of work, particularly if guests come from abroad or travel to a different country, or if the mother organising this just doesn't know the area where the wedding is being held. For all "non-hostess" mothers this becomes an important part of the wedding:

Moira (daughter): "We hosted something the night before. When all the family arrived, we got them all together the night before. I organised that basically. C (daughter) was with us. That felt nice and important."

Helen describes how at her son's wedding she "felt like a guest at a lovely party... I was the hostess though the night before when all the men of the family stayed with us, and breakfast was quite something!"

Louise whose son's wedding is essentially organised by the couple and the daughter-in-law's family: "We invited all my family for a meal the night before the wedding. That was our part."

Marie's daughter is getting married abroad near her new husband's family: "I felt a bit tacked on to events; do you know what I mean? Looking after our own guests, well that was something I could do without feeling I could be accused of muscling in. I felt quite strongly that they all should feel really welcome, maybe because sometimes I felt, I don't know, not entirely welcome myself I suppose. Not as welcome as I would have liked to feel."

This last comment highlights again that the issue here is often not necessarily about wanting to be the hostess, but rather wanting to be welcome and special at their child's wedding.

In this context, being recognised and greeted and maybe complimented by guests at the wedding, treated by them as either hostess or at least a very special guest, matters enormously:

Marie who had not even felt sure about her being a special enough guest at her daughter's wedding declares herself delighted that so many of her daughter's friends whom she had not seen for a while recognised her, seemed pleased to see her and complimented her on her dress. "Several of them said I looked great, and that was so nice, I mean, it's always nice to get a compliment, but it meant more. I felt so pleased that they sought me out and took the trouble."

Angie is also pleased: "Getting comments, 'oh, you've scrubbed up well,' [laughs]."

Barbara (son): "It was lovely being with my family, dancing. I felt fit and well, I got compliments. I really loved my dress. My sister-in-law said, 'you look brilliant'."

Melanie (daughter): "I was so moved by individuals who came and said, 'what a lovely occasion, what a lot of planning you have put into it, you have achieved such a lovely day.' I was included in being part of that."

This last comment shows clearly that the question is one of being included and being a crucial participant at this celebration, whether as official or unofficial hostess or as special guest. The non-hostess mothers had to work harder at this. They may create an event as part of the wedding where they are the hostess or they may take up some hostess responsibilities on the day. On the whole they were significantly more dependent on other people's including and welcoming attitude. Their own guests, their own family, their child's friends and the other family all play a part in this.

Ultimately it is not whether guests see the mother as a special and crucial person at this wedding, but whether her own child is able to give her that confirmation, and it is the occasions when that happens that lead to special moments, as will be seen in the following chapters.

3.2 Getting ready on the day and THE dress revisited

Mothers of the bride have a particular chance of a special role and some private quieter moments around the ritual of getting the bride ready. There is still the old tradition, upheld by all the families in these interviews, for the groom not to see the bride on the morning of the wedding, with the dress being kept a secret from everybody apart from a few people, nearly always women. The mother of the bride has always seen the dress, the bridesmaids have, sometimes, but more rarely, the other mother has. None of the fathers in this sample had. This allows for the "getting ready" to involve only a few people. It often also involves the photographer and another person who will do the bride's and various other people's hair and sometimes make-up. It is a very female and family-of-the-bride dominated part of the wedding. As nearly all families stuck to the other tradition that bride and groom do not spend the night prior to the wedding together, the getting ready happens in the location where the bride spends the last night of her unmarried life, often together with her family of origin. This may be her childhood home, more often a hotel or rented accommodation near the wedding venue. Parents of grooms also tend to stay the night where their son is, but the morning of the wedding is less ritualised and mothers of grooms can indeed feel a bit at a loss what to do:

> Barbara recalls walking a bit aimlessly through the hotel on the morning of her son's wedding, feeling "a bit lost: what am I supposed to do now? a bit twitchy... then later, when my family arrived, I thought, 'oh right, here we are.'"

They may feel quite restricted in what they are allowed to do:

Barbara: "I wanted to be with my son really, but I did not want to over-mother."

Angie recalls the moment of her son arriving at the place of ceremony: "I saw him, we had a hug. I thought his hair was too short and he hadn't shaved properly... of course I didn't say anything."

For mothers of brides the getting ready prior to the ceremony is a big part of the day. Expectations are high and it does not always work quite the way they thought it would:

Beverly remembers it all getting a bit stressful trying to help her daughter to get dressed: "I couldn't do the dress up, there was something wrong at first, then the bridesmaids forgot their bouquets, we were late..."

Maggie also remembers it not going entirely smoothly: "I was a bit rushed and flappy, all fingers and thumbs, but my emotions were quite in check."

Tricia had expected it to be a bit more of an occasion: "I was surprised how little I had to do. It was the bridesmaids really and the make-up lady, they did most of it."

Melanie did actually miss the moment her daughter puts the dress on, as the complicated logistics of using bathrooms and having the hair done for herself and the bridesmaid meant she was not in the room at the time. "So her dad saw her first and I think she wanted it that way."

Suzie recalls: "The most anxiety-provoking moments were for me around the dress. She asked me, could I iron it. How terrifying! I took the ironing upstairs and did it on my own, really quietly... then on the day the zip got stuck. I thought, 'shall I just pull?' I was terrified."

Gemma calls it "the intimate, the dressing bit". "I was trying to build her confidence, but she was motoring by then... it was very short, we didn't have any time to reflect, the bridesmaids were having crises. It was very practical." Was she emotional? "[Laughs], I can't remember." Later she says, "There are times where I would have liked to be with her more, but we were so busy..."

For most of the mothers of daughters something else is happening though. I was struck how many actually used the phrase "getting her dressed" or "dressing her". Even accounting for the elaborate nature of some of the wedding dresses where some help may be needed doing zips up etc., I think the phrase "getting her dressed" does not necessarily refer to the practicalities involved. There is more at stake here. For many mothers this is a moment that links the present to the past, the grown-up bride to the little girl. Being the mother of a small child involves a lot of getting the child dressed, doing their hair. For years these mothers would have been busy doing this every morning, getting their child ready for the day, for school, but also for special occasions like birthday parties or family occasions. Mothers of girls certainly will have memories of party dresses and helping their daughter feel "like a princess" for the occasion. There will have been years of handling their child's little body, being the person who has easy access to the child physically and whose administrations and caresses are mostly accepted and welcome, in fact often sought by and essential to the child. Particularly early motherhood is characterised by this physical dimension and mothers often describe it as a crucial and rewarding aspect of looking after a small child. After nine months of carrying a child there are still years of physical boundaries between mother and child being slightly blurred, with easy physical intimacy being an indication of successful attachment. Gradually this changes. Mothers do recall maybe needing to restrict physical contact when the child's friends are around, and kisses in public may become embarrassing. Privacy needs to be increasingly respected, bathroom doors begin to be locked, bedroom doors require knocking. Mothers need to read their children's signals and respond to them in order to successfully negotiate the right balance between physical expressions of affection and the child's increasing need to have their own privacy and boundaries respected. At the same time physical intimacy may develop for the child with peers and eventually with a sexual partner. The transition has been completed and somebody else now has the intimate easy physical access to their child that once was the mother's domain.

Again, all this has happened for a while; nothing about this is new, but the wedding not only represents and seals this new intimate union, but it also allows, at least for the mother of the bride in the dressing of the bride, a brief recapturing of earlier days. Photographers "know" that, and most photos of this part of the day include a photo of the mother of the bride in physical contact with her daughter, maybe closing some buttons, putting on a necklace, smoothing back a veil.

Jane says with emotion: "She was really keen for me to be there, to dress her." She shows me her "favourite" photo of the wedding, of herself and her daughter, with her daughter leaning into her mother, making herself smaller, moulding into her mother like a small child. "She wanted me be to be there. She said, 'Mum I'm so nervous.'"

Jane is equally emotional: "I helped her get dressed, do all the buttons up, like in the old days."

Marie has not had an easy time in the preparation of the wedding, but she recalls helping to get her daughter ready very fondly: "It was quite odd; we had not done anything like that for a long time, just the two of us in the room. Even standing behind her looking into the mirror, it so reminded me of the days when I would stand behind her and dry her hair or brush it, all those pony tails and plaits... Later the girls would get ready together for a party or going out, but by then I was not part of that anymore."

Mothers of sons are not given these chances. They are left to do a bit of readjusting of flowers in buttonholes, or, in one touching scene, a mother of a son is seen, on a very hot wedding day, to be powdering her son's nose, as the heat or the occasion made him look a bit sweaty!

Mothers of daughters however are given a chance to re-enact a memory. They get their daughter "ready" for the ritual that marks a new bond and a new life, but at the same time there and then they can create an intimate moment that confirms a continuing special bond between themselves and their child. The getting ready becomes a central part of the wedding as a rite of passage, a pivotal point between the past and the future.

3.3 The other family and other territorial issues

There eventually comes the point when the "getting ready" phase comes to an end and the two families and the couple join for the actual ceremony with the couple exchanging vows in front of witnesses and the subsequent celebration.

In Western weddings the guests will have gathered, in a church, a registry office or a registered venue. The groom's party, including his parents, family, ushers, best man and the groom himself will be waiting. The bride's family will also be gathered. Sometimes the protocol of the mother of the bride being the last to enter is observed, signalling that proceedings are about to begin. The bride is the last to appear, in most weddings the father of the bride or a male relative will walk her down the aisle and eventually step back for her to join the groom. The ceremony can begin. From then on the families are mere witnesses to the main event, the joining of the couple saying their vows to each other.

Different cultures have different rituals, some of them placing a different emphasis particularly on the role of the family. Hindu weddings for example involve the family to a much greater degree. The groom will be greeted formally not just by his new parents-in-law, but her whole family will gather behind them. Elders of each family will greet each other; presents will be given not to the young couple but will be exchanged between the two families. In the actual ceremony both sets of parents stand behind their child. They have active roles, such as the symbolic washing of the groom's feet by his new mother-in-law. In fact, as one mother told me, in a good Hindu wedding there should be an active part for every member of the family, even if it consists of both humorous and symbolic acts like the bride's brother twisting the groom's ear! As one interviewee put it:

"There are two families getting married."

Indeed, this may be visible in the subsequent celebration. Both families are likely to be identifiable through some colouring of their dress, men from each family often wearing turbans in identical colours signifying the belonging to one or the other family. The gradual weaving together of the two families can be observed in the gradual mixing of colours in the party scene. Of course, this does not mean at all that the two families get on any better or worse, but it sets an expectation about what *should* be happening at a wedding and what significance the wedding has for the families and not just for the couple.

Nearly all the women I interviewed had had contact with the other family, particularly the other mother, for a while before the wedding. As described in Chapter 2, contact between the two families and two women had been achieved with greatly varying degrees of success and this not surprisingly is mirrored on the day of the wedding.

Often the two families spend a couple of days in the run-up to the wedding together, preparing for the day or in some cases getting to know each other in organised get-togethers:

Barbara spends several days with her son's future parents-in-law and family prior to the wedding which is taking place abroad. "They were such good hosts, there were activities before the wedding and everybody got to know each other."

Monica, whose son is also marrying abroad, is impressed by how the other family have worked on both families getting to know each other prior to the wedding and on the day. There are a series of events, including a riverboat trip with karaoke before the wedding. "We got to know people, it broke the ice."

On the day both these mothers also talk about variations to the wedding ritual that help them to feel involved and linked in with the other family. Barbara finds out at the wedding rehearsal that she is going to walk her son down the aisle which she is very pleased with. Monica is surprised and delighted to find that not only will both parents of the bride walk her down the aisle, but that also she and her husband will walk their son down the aisle. Both weddings take place in North America and these mothers comment on this perhaps being a foreign thing, but both thoroughly approve.

> *Monica (son) describes that on the wedding day all female members of both families had their hair done together and were present for the bride's first showing herself in the dress. In the reception room there is a table with a photo display of family photos, photos of the weddings of parents and grandparents, "the dog of one family and the cat of the other family". After the ceremony there is a quiz at the reception with questions about both bride and groom growing up: "People had to ask each other questions. They came towards you, said 'hello, I am so and so.' It was really nice."*

Both these mothers comment on the effort the other family has made and also on the fact that the weddings take place abroad, suggesting that it is somehow due to a different cultural tradition that the connection between the two families is more emphasised. The same point is made by another mother where the wedding is held in the UK but the other family come from a different country:

> *Angie (son): "What it felt like during the weekend, it was a marriage between two people that also joined two families. It is possibly a bit more Spanish. There is a word in Spanish for what we have become: mothers who are joined through their children... They invited us for Christmas, they said, 'because you are family now'... Her father said in the speech: 'thank you for bringing us all together.'"*

> *Both mothers of bride and groom share their special moments on the day after the wedding: "She and I talked about it the next morning, we both cried buckets."*

These particular mothers stress the unusualness of this strong connection and see it as something nearly foreign.

What matters most in the interactions with the other family is the quality of warmth:

> *Jill's own mother died not long before the wedding and the other mother responds to this immediately. "She immediately said how sorry she was, she told me about her own mother. There was so much warmth." She describes both families mixing and dancing with each other at the wedding.*

> *Monica recalls how the other mother had provided a toy cat for Monica's granddaughter who was a flower girl. She had heard about the family cat being important and "she had remembered that detail, that was so thoughtful."*

> *Barbara comments: "I got on very well with her [daughter-in-law's] mum. She actually said, 'it's like having a sister.' There was no competition. We were both very generous with each other, about how we both looked for example. She even told me about her relationship with her daughter... On the day I felt she was rooting for me, making sure I got a photo taken with my son, even though that had not been on the list."*

> *Helen still feels very emotional when she recalls the actual moment when her daughter-in-law walked into the church on her father's arm: "When they [bride and her father] came into the church, she [mother of the bride] took my hand."*

However, things do not always go that smoothly. If in the build-up to the wedding the relationship between the two families, and particularly the two mothers, has been distant, this is not likely to change now. In some cases there is a clear feeling that both families are having two different and distinct weddings whilst attending the same event. They may deliberately or instinctively blank the other family out of their experience in order to enjoy the day. In fact, some mothers in these interviews do not mention the other family, or only rather in passing, referring to them only as to when they arrived perhaps or where they stayed. In those cases it was necessary to probe a bit more:

Sheila (daughter) is aware of using this strategy. The other mother is described as "nice... it's just, she is very distant, totally involved with her own family, very close, very closed family." On the day, Sheila recalls saying to the other mother: "'I am so excited, my first daughter getting married,' and she said, 'well, it's my first son getting married too.' It was the way she said it, it made me stop talking with her, I turned to the girls and chatted with them..." In fact in the end she feels: "It was like two different parties, there was a short exchange, 'how lovely it was,' but after that the families did not mix... Thinking back, should I have made more of an effort? I just did not want to spoil the feeling, so I blocked them out."

Michele (son) thinks the other family "did not behave very well. They kept to themselves and just glared. Something must have happened for them to glare like that, but I don't know what it was. It wasn't right, they should have supported her [bride] more."

Maggie (daughter) recalls that the groom's brother got very drunk: "He heckled all the speakers... His mother did not have one nice thing to say to about the wedding, didn't say once to my daughter, 'you look nice.' The morning after they literally stood in the doorway, watching us packing up, watching us carrying boxes without lifting a finger."

Melanie (daughter) wonders after the wedding: "I said to my husband 'I'm not sure what happens now.' I sent them an email inviting them to share photos. They eventually mailed back, chatty, as if we had met at somebody else's wedding, nothing about joining as families, pleasant enough..."

Marie who has had very limited contact with the other family prior to the wedding says about her daughter's mother-in-law: "She was polite, but very cold to all of us, quite unbelievable really, I fear that is just the way she is."

Gemma regrets not talking with the other family enough on the day: "I just remember thinking 'I want to talk to my own family now, because we see so little of each other.' I did not talk much to P's [son-in-law's] uncles. I didn't know who they were, but it's a bit odd that they didn't introduce themselves to me. I mean after all they could identify me but I wouldn't know them."

Several mothers comment on a difference in family culture becoming very visible on the day:

Louise (son) says the day "slightly highlighted the difference between the two families. They had their little rituals, dancing around with their tie on their head and their trouser leg rolled up, and I thought, 'oh God, what is my family going to think about that...Class? [laughs]', well there is a bit of a difference. On the whole it felt more like their day. We were like two separate families; they did not introduce their family to us... when the photo book came out afterwards, we were hardly in it, our side."

Marie (daughter) was very aware on the day how "posh" the other family really were: "I had not noticed it that clearly before and I thought, well, that explains a lot, [laughs]."

Aysha is very unhappy about the other family's behaviour on the day: "They came late, not dressed up at all, they sat separately, they did not talk to anybody."

Moments of sadness, jealousy and upset about exclusion may happen at unexpected times. It is as if at this stage these feelings are noted, but set aside on the day:

Diane has felt excluded all the way along and this continues to hurt at moments on the day: "It's the little things; there was no corsage for me. All that expense on buttonholes and pew ends, all that, but I was never asked whether I wanted one."

Tricia (daughter) regrets that "when the pictures were taken nobody said to me, 'come on in, you should be in,' so we have no official family photo with me in it."

Moira talks of "little pangs" that her daughter is getting married from the groom's home: "I had a pang now and again, but it was quite distant. His mother got a couple of her friends to make some biscuits, a bit of a nibble after the ceremony, and I thought, 'oh, who has done these? I bet she has."

Diane feels the other family left her out of things: "There were little things that were hard: herself, her sister and her mother, they had their hair done on the day and I was not included."

Barbara feels the "pang" when she hears her son's in-law family talk about him: "'We did this with him, he said that.' They see so much more of him."

However, these moments in the telling of the wedding day are quickly brushed aside. Even some unpleasant encounters are remembered, but at the time the mothers do not react to them fully. Some talk of rudeness from the other family. There are some not-so-welcome speeches. One mother of a groom tells of the bride arriving at the church on her own, as there seems to have been some argument between mother and daughter and she is upset on behalf of her daughter-in-law. Another mother of a groom finds out on the wedding day that the father of the bride behaved inappropriately towards one of the younger members of her family earlier in the day. In both cases the mothers in question decide to let the incident go, as they don't want to be the one to spoil their child's special day. In fact, they don't allow it to spoil their own experience of the day. One of them says she couldn't allow herself to get really angry at the time, as she wouldn't have known what to do with that. All others who had negative experiences on the day agree that their child should not know about this, partly because they will have to get on with their in-laws beyond the wedding day, but also in order not to taint the magic quality of the day: the memory must be preserved as a good one.

3.4 Choreography of the day: walking down the aisle, speeches and seating plans

The relationship between the two families as it unfolds on the day is acted out against the background of their official roles and positions in the wedding celebration. There is a clear choreography laid out for at least part of the day: decisions on walking the bride "down the aisle", giving speeches and seating plans will have been made well before the day and everybody is going to take their place in it. Many weddings have a rehearsal the day before the ceremony and this highlights the performance aspect of the wedding. Again, what is noticeable is that everybody is aware of an unspoken protocol around how these things "should be done" and any variations on the theme are precisely that: deliberately chosen variations which tend to have meaning for the participants:

> *Shirley, whose daughter is organising the day without involving her mother very much, is concerned: "I knew it in my head that there is a protocol... I wanted to be in charge of that part, so it would be done properly."*

> *Melanie talks about the rehearsal of the wedding ceremony and how the parents of the groom commented several times on proceedings, calling it "a bit of a serious occasion... The word 'properly done, properly,' figured."*

Often the families of origin have already undergone changes themselves, through divorce, perhaps remarriage, the presence of step-siblings. These families will have practised joined occasions like this wedding to various degrees. Still, the allocation of roles on the day needs to be thought through carefully.

A major question is concerned with the arrival of the bride for the ceremony. What nearly all wedding ceremonies seem to have in common is some kind of ritualistic handing over of the bride to the new partner, followed by a stepping back. This may happen prior to the actual marriage ceremony or at some later stage at the end of the celebration, when the bride may be escorted to the groom and the groom's family, as happens in some Muslim weddings. What sometimes is referred to in Western weddings as the father "giving the bride away" may have strong undercurrents of a paternalistic view of the daughter as a near property of her father. However, the stepping back part of the ritual has a psychological and emotional reality.

Walking the bride down the aisle or "giving her away" seems to be, with few exceptions, the prerogative of the biological father of the bride, an emotional moment for the father and for the mother watching it. If the father declines, as happened at two weddings where the previously rather absent father had, true to form, opted out, this is felt to be a very hurtful thing to do to the bride. Often a male relative takes on this role instead. In one case, where the stepfather had been around as an active father for the bride since she was a small child and the biological father had kept regular contact with her throughout her childhood, the family found an ingenious solution: the biological father, who had since trained as a humanist celebrant, conducted the marriage ceremony where he could speak about his daughter. The stepfather on the other hand gave the father-of-the-bride speech and it was the bride's mother who walked her down the aisle. This solution had been arrived at through conversation between all the participants and it sounded like everybody was happy with the outcome. This kind of joint decision does of course not necessarily happen at other weddings.

For the groom, and also for the family and friends gathered, the bride being walked in marks the first sight of her in her wedding dress; for her parents it marks the moment of stepping back: father and daughter come in together, he then stands back for her to join her husband-to-be. In the traditional Western wedding, based on Christian rituals, it is just the father of the bride who performs this symbolic act. However, the theme itself is always present, though in different cultural variations: in Jewish weddings both parents, and indeed the parents of both bride and groom, are part of this ritual of walking their child in and then stepping back. In the Muslim "contract" both parents, who may well have played a strong part in the build-up to the wedding, giving permission and negotiating with the other family, will be there as witnesses to the bride and groom accepting each other as husband and wife. At Hindu weddings the parents continue after this moment to be part of the ceremony. However even then the stepping-back ritual is involved: the bride will enter escorted by her maternal uncles who will then step back. The stepping back may also happen at a later stage of the celebrations:

> Aysha tells of the custom of the female and male guests being separated at the wedding party, but at the end of the party the father of the bride will collect her and take her to her new husband, for the young couple to leave together.

> Meera tells of the bride being escorted to the groom's family towards the end of the celebration. She laughs: "Tears are obligatory." Some brides apparently go as far as enrolling in acting classes in order to perform this ritual convincingly and on cue!

This moment of stepping back holds both ritual and emotional significance. In a way this is the centrepiece of the ceremony and appears not surprisingly as one of the most important special moments. This is after all what many have identified as one of the crucial tasks for the mothers in the build-up to the wedding:

how to be supportive, but at the same time to step back in a deeper and meaningful way. Most of the complicated feelings have been concerned with this task, how it has been facilitated and accomplished, and now it has been done and is enacted in that very moment. Many mothers cry at this stage and the tears prompted by this part of the ritual make more sense when seen in this context, the ritual marking the crucial transition.

Mothers of brides and grooms who are, in the traditional format, relegated to the audience at this stage speak of pride at seeing their child, of joy at seeing them happy. This for many will be one of the special moments that holds a mix of emotions:

> *Irene recalls the moment of seeing her daughter coming down the aisle: "I felt emotional then, more a feeling of relief. The relief that we got there, looking at all these people and thinking: my daughter is safe. I shall feel the loss later."*

> *Alex also remembers being emotional when she sees her husband and her daughter coming down the aisle: "She looked very vulnerable, very young, but then she suddenly grew when they said the vows... in fact they [daughter and son-in-law] were both so adult, organising it all. My little girl, yes, but also so grown up, competent... pride, relief, both."*

> *Marie thought at this same moment: "It's them now, not us any more... not just flown the nest, but building her own as she should, with him, as we did all those years back."*

Marie's comment hints at this dimension of the wedding that ritually links generations: people often do remember their own weddings, parents certainly do. Now it is their child's turn. It is as if a family's history is paused there and then, allowing the mother to feel that past, present and future are coming together at this moment. A new stage of her child's life begins and a stage of her own life has come to a conclusion. It is important to remember that the wedding does not create this: it merely symbolises it. In its visible ritual of the stepping back it is a reminder of an important change that has a powerful impact.

After the actual wedding ceremony the bride's father's official role continues. His next moment of active involvement is the father-of-the-bride speech, an unchallenged centrepiece of the triad of male speeches at the weddings: father of the bride, groom and best man. Women do not have a speaking role, indeed very few seem to question this. Several mothers, both of bride and groom, had been given other speaking parts, mostly readings at the ceremony, with the words chosen for them. Only two women gave a speech at the dinner: one who had brought up her daughter as a single mother and one only after having been asked by her son to do so:

> Monica spontaneously took over when she realised her husband was getting emotional during the speech and had difficulties continuing: "I had not planned to say anything, but when D [husband] spoke I could see he was filling up, so I said, 'do you want me to say something?' and I carried on, reading it out."

Most women did not even know until the day what their husband was going to say in the speech, although some of them had helped him by providing anecdotes. The absence of maternal voices mirrors the bride's silence on this occasion which seemed to be the rule at nearly all the weddings I heard about.

The father-of-the-bride speech tends to follow the format of talking about the daughter, welcoming the new son-in-law into the family and addressing the groom's family in some way. It is supposed to be both emotional and light-hearted and many mothers report tears flowing. The mother will probably have been mentioned, maybe thanked, although that is more the responsibility of the groom, and mothers do remember this happening.

This aspect is rarely however a particularly special moment. What mothers of brides remember more is things like eye contact between father and daughter during that speech and whether the childhood stories and the daughter's reaction to them confirm a special link between daughter and her family of origin.

The father-of-the-bride speech can, within the set format, position various participants in relationship to each other. How genuine and heartfelt are the comments about his daughter? (I did hear mothers who reported that, given their daughter's difficult behaviour in the build-up to the wedding, finding nice things to say about her seemed a bit of a struggle for a while!) How much can the father say about his son-in-law? How much is this person already part of the bride's family? Again, the father may be struggling to find welcoming words when the relationship has been not so smooth. In contrast to that, the mother of the groom may well feel a "pang" hearing her son being claimed by this other family:

> Monica's son married abroad where he has settled: "He [father of the bride] said, 'we do this with Tom, we do that with Tom...' I thought 'that's not fair, but... ok, it's really easy for you to get together...' but then you can't be unhappy if they are happy."

Another aspect of the father-of-the bride speech that mothers commented on was the part that deals with the relationship between the two sets of parents. It was particularly mentioned by the women who had talked about positive relationships with the other parents. Here the speeches can and do go beyond the polite acknowledgements and thanks expressed to the other parents; the other parents are addressed in a clearly affectionate and demonstrative way:

> Angie gives me the speech her son's father-in-law gave at the wedding (in translation from the original Spanish). He starts his

speech with a toast to the family of the groom, and then addresses Angie and her husband: "You are beautiful people, all of you. You have been the other parents to our daughter and ... we cannot show enough all the gratitude we feel for what you have done in looking after her. The friendship and love we have experienced from you and your family has come from the love that has sparked between your son and our daughter."

Jane gets on very well with her daughter's parents-in-law. She says that her husband made a speech that reflected this, "It went beyond just welcoming our son-in-law to our family and thanking them for making our daughter part of theirs. He made a point talking about the parents-in-law, what lovely people they are, addressing them directly by name."

Just like with the getting ready in the morning and the walking down the aisle, mothers of sons are not given any of those rituals in which there is an emphasis on the particular bond between themselves and their child until it is time for their son's speech. However, the groom has a chance to bring his parents back on to the stage and again pride is expressed by mothers indicating that this is a special moment for mothers of sons:

Diane (son): "My son [in his speech when thanking everybody] left me to last: that is the most important one."

Most speeches are given at the sit-down meal for which all guest have their allocated seats, most often with a kind of top table. The seating plan, like other elements of the wedding, has a symbolic significance for the mothers, as became noticeable during the preparations. It allocates family and friends differing degrees of proximity to the wedding couple, and finalising it has often been a difficult part of the wedding preparations. On the day all has been decided, even though feelings about it may still run high. The crucial markers are: who sits at the top table, how mixed are the tables and is there a kind of pecking order between the tables. For the top table there is a protocol which may or may not be observed. The traditional top table would sit the wedding couple together with their parents, the best man and maid of honour. The wedding couple would be flanked by the bride's parents, the bride's mother sitting next to the groom and the father of the groom on her other side. The father of the bride would sit next to his daughter with the groom's mother sitting next to him. The website "Country Bride" suggests various alternatives, including one entitled "avoiding potential friction between bride and groom's parents" which breaks up the dominance of the bride's family by placing the groom's father next to the bride and the bride's mother next to the groom. There are various suggestions for "Bride's or groom's parents divorced and remarried" or "Both sets of parents divorced and remarried", but essentially they follow the assumption that it is close family only at the top table apart from the best man and maid of honour, with the latter two being placed furthest from the wedding couple.

Few weddings that I heard about followed the tradition to the book, but most tried to have close family on the top table. This sometimes posed quite difficult questions as far as divorced or remarried parents were concerned:.

Gina: "It will be a very long top table, [laughs]."

From the mothers' point of view the crucial question was their own presence near their child. There was only one mother who told of a seating arrangement that positioned the young couple with her new in-law family and the mother was left to sit at a different table with the father of the bride and the grandparents. This mother was very upset about the arrangement. Nearly all weddings observed the family-over-friends rule. There were however a few who had friends at the top table, and indeed placed best man and maid of honour between themselves and the parents. Just as in the run up to the wedding and its struggles of where and how the parents, particularly the mothers, are allowed to be involved, this seating order makes another statement about the importance of friends versus family. This statement is repeated in the number of guests drawn from family and peer group friends. In the last generation, the mothers' generation, weddings, if they were formally celebrated at all, had a majority of family on the guest list, with only a few peer friends of the wedding couple. This has clearly changed, with friends of the couple being strongly represented. As discussed in Chapter 2.3 ("who is invited and who does the inviting?"), many mothers have struggled with the little input they were allowed as far as the guest list was concerned, and many of them wished they had been allowed to invite any or more of their own friends or family. This now becomes reactivated around the seating plan.

Some weddings, particularly those that take place in barns in accordance with the current fashion for country weddings, have tables that are clearly closer or further away from the top table, and the importance that is given to various groups of guests is clearly visible. Weddings where round tables are arranged in a circle do not do that to the same extent. Mothers showed me seating plans: if there is clearly visible proximity or distance, then family tend to sit closer to the couple than the couple's friends. There was only one wedding where this seating order had been reversed completely, with family sitting furthest away, mirrored by the best man and maid of honour sitting closer to the couple at the top table than the parents. Interestingly enough, whilst this may have aroused strong feelings in the build-up, even those mothers who had been upset about aspects of the seating arrangements, don't really re-visit this in their account of the day. The original upset may still shine through though:

Maggie (son): "They couldn't have made it clearer really where family figured for them. I was so angry and upset at first when I

*saw the plan. I mean, my elderly mother, his grandma, was sitting
right next to where the disco was going to be later, and she could not
really see them during the meal at all, she was so far away. I couldn't
believe it, but then she [grandmother] left early anyway, and in the
end nobody seemed to mind, or at least they did not say. It was a great
day in the end, in spite of all of it."*

Some seating plans mix up family and friends, thereby getting round
this potential hierarchy, and some seating plans deliberately mix
up the two families. However, there was no particular correlation
between such seating arrangements and how the families got on
with each other on the day in the group of mothers that I spoke
with. That clearly had more to do with what had happened prior to
the day and could not be made much better or worse by a seating
arrangement.

What was striking was the fact that, whilst a lot of effort and
emotional energy had gone into the seating plan, the women I spoke
to had difficulty remembering quite where everybody, including
themselves, had been sitting in the end. It sounded like the reality
of the seating arrangements was in the end a lot less important
than the symbolic significance that they were given in the build-up
to the wedding. Like so many other aspects of the wedding, the real
question was how the couple through these visual arrangements
positioned themselves in relation to their families and how much
significance this bond with their families was given. In that sense
I do not think that these women had been overreacting to the
seating arrangements; I rather think that they were instinctively
responding to the potential meaning that practical arrangements
have in this ritual of transition: in that context their reactions
make perfect sense.

3.5 Special moments and making memories

Weddings are occasions which in our culture are hardly imaginable without some kind of recording of the day, whether this is carried out by a member of the party or, these days more commonly, by a professional photographer. There may be videos or stills: all of them will have a series of photos of the couple, preferably against a picturesque background, some of them of the couple with their families in various combinations. Most photographers nowadays seem to arrive before the actual ceremony and take photos of the story of the day, including the ritualistic "getting ready" of the bride, but also of some near-iconic items: there will be shots of the dress on a hanger, of the shoes, the bridal flowers, any jewellery worn by the bride. There are other iconic moments that tend to be captured by the photographer: the father of the bride walking her in, perhaps part of the ceremony itself, then the couple walking away from the place of ceremony, with confetti and guests surrounding them. These are meant to be the special moments and there is no question that most mothers in these interviews were eagerly awaiting the photos. Many of them were often already exchanging informal photos via Facebook or receiving them from friends and family. The photos were giving them a chance to pore over the day, relive some of the moments, or indeed see part of the wedding day that they had not been part of. The story of the wedding day as told by the photographer allowed them to share the story not just with others, but also with each other again. It allows for those conversations: "Do you remember when...?" and: "Oh, I did not know that was happening at the same time," and it allows the family to confirm to each other again what sort of a day it was. Wedding photos can be displayed and after a while they become part of the story that the family tells itself: this is who we are, this is what we did together, we are a family having passed this particular marker in our family's life cycle:

Diane keeps looking at the photos of her daughter's wedding: "We still look at the photos a lot, just looking at the memories."

Shirley compares it with past events when "making memories" was a crucial part of the experience, and a milestone in the family's story was marked: "We did a trip to India together when my daughter was younger, we made memories, we made our milestones memories, and with this wedding we'll have to do that again. It is not easy, but we need to make it into a good memory."

Some mothers however did mention the photographer's presence as disruptive, particularly when the photographer is present in those more private moments, like for example when the bride is getting ready. What became very apparent either way was that the moments the mothers mentioned as special moments were not necessarily at all the ones highlighted by the photographic records, and indeed not necessarily the ones that they themselves expected: they were often moments of pause between active phases. Nearly all of them were moments that held a more personal and intimate connection with their child:

Suzie's daughter had a registry office ceremony a couple of days before the official wedding day. This first ceremony was only open to immediate family and she feels that this was the day that held most intimacy for her: "Intimate moments are never when you expect them to be. They take you by surprise, they are your own intimate moments... By the time it's all going on you give up on intimacy. It becomes a group event, there is an audience... the registry office ceremony: we all felt it, that it was so precious that we had this quiet family intimate ceremony where it was just us, where everybody there was so closely connected to the bride and groom. And it was all so private. That little ceremony, so emotionally charged, that for me was when she got married."

Melanie mentions as a special moment when her daughter after the rehearsal in the church the day before the wedding, which included future parents, parents-in-law, bridesmaids, best man etc, says to her mother: "'I just want to go home now', and it was just us, my two daughters, and the bridesmaids, a low key evening, it felt right." Another important moment she mentions is when her daughter at the moment of signing the registry, after exchanging the vows, makes eye contact with her.

Several mothers mention eye contact, at the moment of walking into the place of ceremony, during a speech, before setting off. Some talk about the time of getting their daughter ready.

Jill describes how her daughter said on the morning of the day: "'Mum, I've got a surprise for you at the wedding'... so then later she arrives with her father and when they walk down the aisle they play 'God only knows' by the Beach Boys. I am a massive fan, that is my song, and they played that when she came down the aisle. I was in floods of tears, she had done that for me, that's the girl she is. That was her little thing for me."

Monica's son got married abroad and she was not particularly involved in any planning for the wedding. She did not mind and yet she is pleased when she notices the couple's choice of music for the first dance: "We all had to send in a special song and they chose the one that I had sent for their first dance."

Beverly recalls a special moment just before she leaves her daughter at the church: "That last minute before she was going to go into church, it was just me, her and the bridesmaids, that last minute, it was just us; that was lovely."

Marion similarly remembers a last private moment: "When I was picked up to go to the church when I saw her standing in the kitchen and I kissed her goodbye... [cries]."

Diane's son is seeking his parents out on his own at several occasions during the wedding; Michele is hugged in front of everybody by her son and daughter-in-law after reciting a poem; Angie shares a joke with her son before the ceremony about fiddling and how this will be the last time she nags him; Helen is hugged for a long time by her daughter-in-law.

What all these mothers experience as special intimate moments is based on their child's drawing a momentary circle around the two of them or at least around the small family group, an acknowledgement of a special bond at this moment of rite of passage:

Helen (son): "I felt welcome, more than that, I felt like someone who was loved."

That this is indeed a rite of passage is also highlighted in those special moments. Mothers are looking backwards and forwards and their emotions are often about a sense that their child has arrived at this place of adulthood, about to take up their place in the next generation of adults and perhaps parents in this family. Sometimes there is an overwhelming sense of relief that their child has reached this relative place of safety and so has their relationship:

Angie had times when she had worried a lot about her son: "Yes, there was a sense of loss; this is not my little boy any more, but, more so, I was so proud, a sense of him being ok, after all that happened... I talked to a close friend of B [son] and he said that B was ok. He lost his way for a while and for me there is a lot of relief. I am very thankful."

Jane also remembers that things have not always been easy for her daughter: "It was such a proud moment, she was so happy. Out of all my children she has found life a bit harder, and now she was so happy."

Tricia feels relief: "To see how everybody had made such an effort for her, how they hold her in such high regard." She then likens it to a "coming together, like after a war, I felt peaceful", and when asked about the image of the war, she elaborates: "So much could have gone wrong, for her, for our relationship, but she has come through unscathed. She has now got this far, she is settled, she is ok now."

Helen echoes this feeling: "To see all his friends and what an effort they had made for him, how special he is to them."

Another type of special moment is often about seeing the family together, not just the inner family, but people who have been part of this family's history:

Beverly recalls the moment she walked into the church: "I walked in and all of a sudden ... I knew all these people, it really hit me, I knew all these people."

Monica says the highlight was "seeing all our family and friends together. We were in a pub... and I looked around me, my children, my family, friends, they were all there."

Barbara comments on the pleasure of seeing her sons together: "It was just lovely being with my family."

Marie also feels that it was important that people who were part of the family's history came together for the occasion of the wedding: "There were people on our side who have been part of our life for so long, but not all of them have known each other, and there everybody was, together. That was really important."

This latter sentiment is echoed by several mothers who in turn may have had very small weddings, so this new wedding has been sometimes the first opportunity for members of their own and their own in-law family to meet each other.

This may be why mothers who were not "allowed" enough family or family friends as guests feel that something is missing:

> Monica talks about a neighbour's child's wedding: "It was just all about the young couple's friends, not even their [parents] closest friends were invited, quite selfish really."

> Louise has regrets: "We had very few of our friends there. In hindsight I should have stuck out for more people on our side."

I don't think this is just about sharing this particular occasion with close people, but also about an awareness of time pausing, allowing a moment where the history of this particular child and this particular mother are re-viewed and re-experienced. If the couple's friends and the other family represent the future, then having people present at the wedding who were part of this history is about marking and acknowledging the past and giving it a proper place at this momentous occasion.

Chapter 4

Time Travel

So far I have concentrated on themes that all the interviews had in common, concerned with undercurrents that would have been relevant to all the mothers I spoke with, whatever their cultural background and their particular family story. It seems indeed that there is no such thing as a wedding that does not involve, to varying degrees, experiences such as transition, change, loss, rivalry, but also joy, love, pride, acceptance, feelings of inclusion and exclusion. One way or the other all women referred to those experiences, and some themes were stronger for some women than for others. Of course, some mothers had an easier time than others, some mothers managed these times better than others, some women were more able to express their feelings than others, but all of them had to deal with these themes in their own way.

What I have not approached yet is the question of how the individual differences between these mothers can be explained in more detail.

What was apparent with all the women I talked with was that their reactions and expectations, particularly at the early stage of imagining the wedding, were embedded in patterns of previous experience which were re-emerging, having been triggered by this new event. After all, if themes like transition, loss, rivalry and separation form the difficult background to weddings, then these themes are by their very nature not something that any of these mothers would have had to deal with for the first time. Earlier experiences would feed into the experience of the wedding.

Not surprisingly one of the main patterns was the character of the relationship with the child in question and how the wedding activated this relationship with its special features. Given that a wedding symbolises a step in the child's journey to independence and separateness from the parent, I asked all the mothers to remember other steps of this journey: maybe their child's first day at school, or the move to secondary school, the beginnings of adolescence with its emphasis on separation, leaving home, maybe going to university. What interested me was whether there was a connection between how those transitions had been experienced and managed in the specific past of this mother and this child and what was happening now in this transitional event of a wedding.

I also asked the mothers to remember how these stages had been managed in their *own* growing up and how this compared. They talked about themselves as mothers in this process, but also as daughters in their separation from their own mothers. So the other relevant pattern was the quality of their own relationship with their mothers and their own growing up into independent adulthood. I was interested to see whether there were any noticeable parallels and links between those experiences and a particular mother's account of the wedding of her child.

Indeed, each story that I heard seemed to be held together by a strong thread linking being a daughter with being a mother and now a mother-in-law, linking the past with the future with the wedding being a pivotal moment in the middle.

In science fiction and fantasy fiction there is the device of the time portal, allowing characters to be transported into the past or the future. Weddings seem to be such portals of the psyche, allowing the participants access to other emotionally significant events in their own and their family's lives. Sometimes these connections are made quite consciously, but at times they appear rather hidden in the fabric of the interviews.

As an analytic psychotherapist I am trained to listen out for these parallel themes and associations, but of course the women in the interviews were not engaging with me as a psychotherapist, and neither had they given me permission to explore or interpret these themes in more depth. The following observations, whilst going deeper into some individual stories, are therefore cautious and tentative.

As outlined before, all names have of course been changed and so have various details of the stories, keeping only what is necessary to make the pattern in question visible.

Viv

Viv and I talk about her son's wedding in the sitting room of Viv's town house overlooking the park. The room is furnished with antique and modern furniture, clearly carefully chosen. There is a piano in the corner, the walls are lined with books, and there are beautiful objects displayed throughout: the room feels like an oasis of taste and cultured serenity. Viv seems to be enjoying the interview, talking about the forthcoming wedding with an air of amused detachment. Her son, a professional musician, is marrying a young woman whose family has embraced the wedding preparations with some enthusiasm. It is going to be a traditional big wedding dominated by the bride's family. Neither Viv not her son seem to be much involved in any of the planning; in fact Viv has refused an invitation to look with her future daughter-in-law at a wedding dress, because she finds the whole excitement about things like that slightly "naff". In fact, the whole wedding and everything that she has heard about it feels slightly naff to her: the money involved, the "celebrity wedding" style ("there will be doves, no doubt!"), and though it is never directly said, her daughter-in-law seems to be included in this description. She is described as nice and competent, but words like talented, intelligent, sophisticated are reserved for her son. Viv would have wished for something else for him, and again, whilst this comment refers to the wedding, I can't help but feeling this may extend to her future daughter-in-law too, who seems to be rather damned with faint praise.

Only further into the conversation do I hear about Viv's own first marriage to her son's father: he was seen by his parents as the intelligent, cultured and sophisticated party and at that time it was Viv whose competence and niceness was clearly seen by them as inferior and the marriage as a bit of a compromise. Further back in her childhood there is also an older brother who was their parents' favourite. A working-class family, they adored and indulged this son who was the first in his family to go to university. Viv also went to university, but this seems to have been noticed less. Her role in her family of origin was to be the one who did not cause any trouble or excitement.

Any hurt about this is only hinted at and, if talked about at all, then again it is in a tone of slightly amused detachment. It is clear that both this detachment and a fierce determination to become the truly intelligent, successful, talented and sophisticated one in this competition have been Viv's coping devices. "Golden boy" brother did not do so well after all, and Viv's ex-husband's business ventures failed one after the other in spite of his "brilliance". It is Viv who has created this life and this room and she is at ease with it: it is hers.

The wedding and her attitude to it could then be seen as another way of re-visiting a past conflict, only this time with reversed roles. This time it is Viv, who through her son is on the side of "golden boys", in a position to safely look down, rather than be looked down upon. It allows her in a subtle way to rewrite history. I do not think that Viv is aware that this may be what she is doing, but she nevertheless draws satisfaction and relief from being on the other side, reversing a painful and traumatic pattern of her past.

The next example is Helen who has also found a way of using the wedding to readdress unresolved issues of the past by reversing earlier experiences. Helen however, unlike Viv is very aware of the fact that the wedding gives her chance to replay something, but this time with a totally different quality, reversing an earlier painful pattern.

Helen

Helen's wedding was, in her own words, a nightmare. Neither her own nor her husband's family were prepared to make an effort to get on with each other and nobody seemed to be the slightest bit concerned whether this would be a happy event for Helen:

> *"I remember it as a horrible day. I put so much effort into it to make something happen, bring people together: a complete and utter waste of time!"*

This was not that surprising to her, given that she seems to have always been the "parental child" in her family: she was the competent daughter, successful at school, sensible and popular with friends and teachers, "head girl material". What neither her friends nor her teachers knew was that Helen, during and after her parents' divorce, became effectively her mother's carer. Her mother fell apart when the marriage came to an end and Helen often did not attend school, as she was too anxious to leave her mother on her own. Eventually her mother remarried, but at any point in her mother's life when things became difficult, Helen was called upon to provide support, often speaking with her mother several times a day, coming home for weekends from her university course. Her mother would easily feel excluded when Helen's life became fuller, and her demands would increase. Mother's self-centredness is remembered in Helen's recollections of Mother's talking about Helen's future:

> *"She said: 'I hope you will provide me with a grandchild one day,' not: 'I hope you will have children one day.' That was the way it was between us."*

Her husband's family does not provide much relief: whilst they do give practical support during the time when Helen's three children are young and she continues to work full-time, they are not the kind of family who value fun or playfulness. Physical contact is not something that comes easily to any of them. Helen can fit in, as her own work ethic fits in very well with that of her new family, but life stays "heavy" and is described as fairly relentless. Some of her description of family life just reflects the pressures of working full-time and bringing up a family, but there is an extra dimension to it, an expectation that this is naturally her lot. Helen has moved near her in-law family and that way has managed to get away from her mother's demandingness, if at a price, namely constant guilt and an expectation that one day she will be punished for this act of "selfishness". She describes early motherhood as ambivalent:

> "I always needed to get back to work. I was always somebody who could very happily watch her children sit on somebody else's lap. It was lovely with them when they were small, but there was always the weight of responsibility."

Here too she expects punishment:

> "When they were little I did not fear losing them, but now I do."

Now her eldest son is getting married and Helen has for a long time predicted and feared that this will mean that he will join another family and leave her behind, just as she did with her own mother. Families cannot share, children cannot wait to get away, and her own selfishness will now be punished at last: this is clearly the script that Helen expects to be acted out:

> "I have feared that all my life, that the girls will take our boys away, you know, where only the family of the girl matters. I have thought that to be likely, I wouldn't have been surprised."

However, something extraordinary happens. The new daughter-in-law is reaching out to Helen in a warm and genuine way, including her in all preparations:

> *"She just warms your heart. I only need to see her and I feel good... she puts her arm through mine, I hug her, she hugs me. That's not the family we are, we don't hug, but she has brought that into our family."*

The other family is equally inviting and warm, and the two families actually get on like a house on fire. So now Helen is:

> *"holding my breath".*

In her description of the forthcoming wedding, talking about being invited by her future daughter-in-law to be involved, about looking forward to the wedding and meeting her son's old and new friends, there is one word that features repeatedly: this wedding is going to be "carefree", a concept that does not describe much of her life so far. It is not surprising that this is a wedding that is experienced nearly as a reconciliation with fate. She is not religious but she uses the phrase

> *"as if God is giving me something back".*

I am not sure whether this refers to being given a sort of reward for all she has done, or whether it refers to something that she had been robbed of when young. Whichever interpretation is closer to what she means, it is clear that this wedding is repairing something for her in a deeply meaningful way.

Something is lifting for Helen and she discovers sides to herself that were not available to her before in that way, an outrageous side, frivolous, playfully experimenting:

"At a party recently I was really flirtatious, cheeky. I have never done that before, some of my friends are very surprised. Quite safe, you know, playing... I am getting in touch with my inner floosy! [laughs]."

Is this a particularly nice wedding preparation and wedding? Probably, but the point is that something about the specific inclusive and "carefree" quality of it finds a very specific place and heals a very specific wound in Helen. Helen knows this and embraces it.

This wish to reverse something, to replay something, but this time with a difference, is there in quite a lot of mothers, more or less close to the surface. It is as if the past is again catching up with them and they are aware that it influences their experience of this wedding. Sometimes it allows for a healing resolution, like for Helen and Viv. Sometimes though the painful pattern is just being replayed. In those cases seemingly trivial things gain an emotional power that otherwise does not make much sense. Carole is a good example of this.

Carole

After the early death of her father, Carole's mother remarried, and Carole was brought up by her mother and stepfather. Soon afterwards her twin stepbrothers were born and Carole was sent to boarding school. Throughout her childhood she struggled with a vague sense of being the outsider and having to be "good" to be included. She got on well enough with her stepfather, but her relationship with her mother never quite recovered. For a long time she felt a strong dislike for her mother, whilst at the same time feeling the need to please her. There are a variety of factors that make Carole's experience of her daughter's wedding difficult: the dominance of the other family and her daughter's behaviour, which Carole experiences as lacking in consideration and at times downright hostile. The degree of her distress makes more immediate sense when seen in the context of her childhood. Her daughter is not just seen as difficult in the build-up to the wedding, but Carole fears that the relationship between her and her daughter is heading the way she knows a mother/daughter relationship can, namely towards a continuing dislike of each other:

> *"I sometimes see her look at me, and that look scares me. When she was a teenager, I knew that look, but now it is back, and maybe it will stay. I remember looking at my mother like that..."*

She is also deeply concerned about getting it wrong, as her emotional script allows for only one reason for this alienation between a mother and a daughter to happen: she herself has not been good enough.

Beyond that, her experience tells her that when there is a rival for love, whether it was little stepbrothers once, or the other family now, you can indeed lose out. They can send you away and you will only be able to watch the new happy family from the outside. Is it really that surprising that Carole's anxiety levels are high when it comes to this wedding? Ultimately the explanation for Carole's feelings does not lie in her daughter's behaviour, difficult as that may be, nor in her relationship with the other family, dominant as they may be. It is the quality of Carole's past experiences that make her see and feel parallels. It is the emotional charge of these parallels that make the wedding and the "stress" surrounding it a lot less manageable than they may otherwise have been.

In Carole's, Viv's and Helen's stories the past and their relationship with their own parents, specifically with their own mothers, is strongly visible. This mother/daughter theme is nearly always present in many variations, sometimes more hidden in the details of the story. Without exception, it influences what each woman brings to the experience of the wedding, not always in a troubling way, but repeated patterns show up again and again.

Monica

Monica is remarkably relaxed about the whole thing. She has recently retired from a successful and demanding career, has already seen one of her five children get married and seems not to be phased by anything. She fills me in briskly on the biographical details of the other members of her family. This is somebody who is used to running meetings efficiently, I remember thinking. It is her son who is getting married and the wedding is going to be abroad where the young couple have settled already. I wonder how she feels about this, but she cheerfully downplays the impact:

> "Well, it could be Australia, but where it actually is, we can fly out and be there the same day."

She is very unsure in our first interview what her function on the day is going to be, and resolutely refuses any suggestions that she could organise the rest of her family for the wedding as far as coordinating flights and accommodation is concerned, as so many other mothers in her situation seem to do:

> "They are all adults; they can arrange their own accommodation."

I don't get the impression that this is a woman who is pretending that nothing important is happening; she is fully aware that her son's decision to marry and settle abroad will have an effect on how family life will continue. Her way of dealing with this becomes clearer to me when she talks about her own childhood. She is the only child of a mother who had a difficult time giving birth to her and who was told she could not have any more children. Subsequently her mother was in a state of constant anxiety about her daughter. Monica does not want to be that kind of mother and has put a lot of effort into avoiding it:

> *"She was always frightened: I was not allowed to ride a bike, to go into town. She still always needs to know where everybody is, what they are doing, even the dogs. I was determined not to be like that, to let them [children] go and be independent."*

Monica is very much looking forward to a distinct couple activity with her husband prior to the wedding: a road trip. Separation from her children is seen on the background of having her own separate life:

> *"I have a career and a good group of friends."*

She has developed competent distancing strategies, such as reminding herself of positive aspects of the geographical distance ("could have been Australia") and organising a separate party at home after the wedding. There may be, as a result of that, also a slight difficulty in exploring her own feelings, as if that was not allowed or may lead to slightly more complicated areas. However, Monica has quite deliberately chosen to allow her children the separate life that she herself had to fight so hard for.

She is deliberately and consciously stepping back and has done so for a while. The wedding prompts her to activate that strategy yet again: Monica the daughter has taught Monica the mother what she must do. Now she does it without needing to think about it: it has become second nature.

In the following example of Beverly, Beverly the daughter has also taught Beverly the mother, but this time the lesson is a different one.

Beverly

Beverly is having a wonderful time preparing her daughter's wedding. There is very little doubt that Beverly is the one who will be organising this wedding, that this is what her daughter wants. They will be managing just fine, why wouldn't they? She describes this daughter as the easy one of her children, as she herself in turn was the easy child, her other child and her own sister occupying the position of the difficult child. She describes happily how her daughter declared very early on after the announcement of the engagement:

"Mum, you are in charge."

It is fascinating to hear later on in the conversation that Beverly describes herself as her own mother's "right hand woman" from the age of three! She is comfortable with the role of supporting her mother and now her daughter, put by both of them in the position of being in charge: this is what she knows and what she does best. Talking about her own wedding the same formulation turns up again:

"I was in charge. My mum does not really do practical support."

She knows what to do when being put in charge and is in fact cherishing the chance to be "right hand woman" once more, this time her daughter's. Beverly has not planned this or worked this out consciously as a strategy. It has become second nature to her and the wedding provides the opportunity to do something again that she can do well and has been rewarded for in the past. To be her mother's support from such an early age would be something that would certainly have had its costs, but it also gave her a clearly defined role, approval and a sense of being important. The daughter who is getting married now allows Beverly to follow this pattern again, and Beverly cherishes the opportunity to be important to her daughter, and the role and approval that comes with: being her daughter's active support.

There are strong parallels in the next example. Beverly has learned early in her life that being in the supportive role gives you a strong and important identity which she can apply without difficulty to the task of the wedding. Barbara in the next example, like Beverly, takes her strategy in dealing with the wedding straight out of her rule book of childhood:

Barbara

Barbara talks about her own childhood:

> *"I really learned very early on not to make a fuss and to get on with it."*

In her reaction to the wedding there is a clear echo of that: competent, slightly distant, managing well. The role of the mother of the groom who is often expected "not to be that fussed" merges with the role of the child who has learned not to make a fuss,

> *"because that was the way to please my mother".*

In all these examples it is essentially the mother/daughter link and the lessons from their own childhood that teaches these mothers how to deal with this new challenging event, whether they know it or not. They apply what they used to do as daughters of mothers to now being mothers of daughters and sons.

There is a different set of parallels that can be observed in the mothers' stories that have more to do with the more recent past. It is often a feature of the relationship between this particular mother with this particular child, something that certainly well precedes the wedding, that can make an appearance in the mother's account of her experience of the wedding. Mothers will have practised how to allow this particular child to become independent, how to deal with conflict with this particular child, whether to expect to be included or excluded by this particular child, to name a few relevant areas. In the following example the theme of "practising" turns up both explicitly and implicitly in the mother's experience of the wedding.

Amanda

Amanda's attitude towards the wedding of her daughter is relaxed and thoughtful. She knows that weddings are, among other things, about separation and knows also that this can create difficult feelings. She is also very clear that she may be better equipped to deal with this, because she had to learn how to deal with separations from her children all her life as a mother. Her children went to boarding school and the divorce from their father led to the children leaving her repeatedly to stay with their father from an early age. She has learned how to engage in some acting that allowed her to deal with the pain of separation, indeed refers to it as "practising":

> *"It was very hard, but I practised to let somebody else take care of her."*

> *"I know what it feels like and maybe that is why I am quite often close to tears at the moment... In a way this wedding is just more of the same."*

She recalls taking her children to meeting points where she would hand them over to their father, remembering the pain of it, but also concluding that in the end she and her ex-husband managed this situation as well as possible. This mother tells me about the part of the wedding ritual that involves her daughter being walked down the aisle. The father of the bride will conduct the ceremony, the stepfather will give the father of the bride speech, but it is Suzie who will "give her daughter away", in an echo of all those handovers years ago:

> "I woke up one morning and I thought: 'I want to give my daughter away.'"

There is a fascinating detail to this: something happens on the day during this part of the ceremony that was unplanned but makes beautiful sense in the light of Suzie's practising. Normally the "giving away" ritual means that the bride is led towards her future husband and the father of the bride, or in this case the mother, places the bride's hand into the groom's, or just steps back leaving the bride standing next to him. When Suzie shows me a little video of this part of the ceremony, this is however not what happens. When she walks towards the groom, the father of the bride, who will conduct the ceremony, steps forward, and Suzie places her daughter's hand into her father's hand who then in turn leads his daughter one step further to the groom. Suzie at that point steps back. Without having planned that detail, both parents perform a ritual that directly echoes what they used to do over the years:

> "Coming in with her and bringing her to him and handing her over... We have done that kind of thing for years. I walked her towards her father, he walked towards me, and I handed her hand to him, and we kissed. It felt really nice."

It is fascinating to see that this is not what either parent planned, nor is it what Amanda described to me. It was only seeing the little video that revealed this detail: a repetition that Amanda was not even aware of.

Often the parallels are multi-layered: the strategies used around the wedding hold echoes of the relationship between this mother and her child during earlier years, but at the same time echoes of this mother's own childhood. Julia is a good example of this.

Julia

Julia has also practised distance from her son through years of boarding school and her subsequent relationship with him as an adult; however her strategies are quite different from Suzie's. When the children went off to school she felt:

> "Great, somebody to take them off my hands, [laughs], go and tidy up the cupboards, read a book, [laughs]."

The son who is now getting married went to boarding school:

> "He has not lived with us since thirteen, so the potential for conflict was so much smaller. When they came home from school, we were just so pleased to see each other. Conflict... the school had to deal with that."

She is hardly involved in the wedding and is at ease with this.

> "I had hardly any time to get worked up about it. There certainly was no explosion of emotion ... I was very close with him when he was a little boy, but now, it's not like that anymore... I did not think [about the wedding] 'this is my baby leaving'. It wasn't going to be a lifestyle change. They had been together for a long time."

Indeed, it seems that the leaving and the "lifestyle change" happened a long time ago. The non-involvement in the wedding parallels a distance that was comfortably established a long time ago. She recalls her daughter's first days at boarding school. Her daughter got very upset and wanted to come home:

> "But matron said, 'look here R [daughter], your parents can't continue running after you; they have their own lives to lead. You just have to knuckle down to it, and she did, [laughs]... It was hard though whenever they went back after holidays."

Julia remembers her own childhood:

> "I was the first in my family to go to university and that was it. No looking back after that."

She describes her own mother as "not close, to be honest", and says about her mother-in-law:

> "She did not approve of me, too much of a hippie. We were very different people, not much in common."

Again, she seems totally unperturbed by the distance. Distance seems to be her coping mechanism of choice in dealing with separations and endings, both in her own family of origin and in her life as a mother. The wedding and her dealing with it reflect this perfectly.

A last example demonstrates how the mother's relationship with her child and the wider context of the mother's life and family history colour the experience of the wedding day.

Denise

Denise has brought up her daughter as a single mother and her daughter's wedding marks a transition that is mainly associated with feelings of relief and pride:

> "Job done! This is the end of my responsibility, the end of my journey."

She feels satisfaction and gratitude:

> "Satisfaction that it has turned out right. It could have gone wrong, but it didn't. Thank you, God: gratitude. So much relief, so much letting go, so much job done."

However, there is another theme running in parallel: Denise is aware of the fact that her daughter has been her significant other for quite a while:

> "I haven't got a plus one... I would have liked somebody there for me [at the wedding]; normally that would have been her... she has always been the one to fill the gap."

The description of the day is punctuated by her awareness of the absence of certain people, for example siblings, who were not there on the morning of the wedding when her daughter was getting ready:

> "They should have been there, for me."

The same is felt at the arrival at the venue:

> "I was expecting my family to be there waiting for me, but there was no space for them."

Her sitting on her own is matched by the daughter's walking down the aisle on her own.

Interestingly at this wedding there is a display of photos of couples in both families who have stayed together, emphasising the couple bond, not surprising after all at a wedding. Yet this leaves out Denise, as she is no longer with her daughter's father. In contrast to that there is Denise's own emphasis on the bond between sisters, aunts, herself and her daughter, balancing it with her joy for her daughter:

> "We are very close, we will never be parted, never be separated, this will not come between us ... I feel the loss now, of course, but seeing the two of them together, that was lovely."

All these mothers fall back on what they have "practised", as Suzie puts it, in their relationship with this particular child and further back in their relationships with their own parents and siblings. They all seem, consciously or unconsciously, to use these patterns of feeling and behaving again in their coping with the wedding.

What do these stories tell us and what light do they shed on the nature of these mothers' experiences?

It seems that for all these women their own experiences around separation, inclusion and exclusion, difference, distance and closeness with their child, but also with previous relevant others, particularly their own parents, are re-triggered by the wedding. In my work as a psychotherapist I would think of it as what is called transferential repetitions. Feelings, expectations, thoughts and behaviours that originally belong to another time and another relationship can get activated if a situation has sufficient parallels to the original situation or relationship. In the consulting room psychotherapists observe this and draw attention to it, but it is not a phenomenon restricted to the consulting room: it happens in life all of the time. Trigger events like weddings may lead to reactions that are characterised by the slight sense of inappropriateness that transferential reactions often have. They may feel or sound over the top given the nature of the trigger, and the person in the grip of it may well be at a loss to explain quite why they react the way they do. This is precisely what many of the mothers describe. They are often taken by surprise and are rather puzzled by their own reaction. To understand what may be going on is not always easy for any of the participants. Some of the mothers already knew, some discovered something new about themselves during the interviews, and some just did not want to explore this in any way. What would be described in the consulting room as defence or resistance was naturally present in some women more than in others, but it would not have been appropriate to interpret or challenge this in these interviews. However, repetitive patterns functioning as coping devices in the face of a challenging or potentially painful situation could be clearly observed in most of these stories. Whether a particular woman tried to take control, to please, to develop distance, to appease or avoid, to deliberately reverse a pattern or to repeat it: there seemed to be as many ways of responding as there were individual women. Each woman facing this new situation of the wedding would naturally use what she had learned to use before: sometimes this was successful and appropriate for the new situation, sometimes it did not work so well. Some women were very aware of this, for others it only emerged indirectly in the story. None of them had entire control over it and for all of them it strongly influenced and coloured the nature of their feelings and reactions.

In the consulting room I am used to the fact that understanding such patterns can bring relief and often be the beginning of change. I was therefore not surprised that in these interviews, which were not meant to be therapeutic in nature but were nevertheless exploring such patterns and repetitions, there were often moments of surprise and relief.

Interviewees declared themselves surprised, amused, but sometimes shocked and taken aback, when I occasionally pointed out parallels that I had noticed. Did this influence their subsequent experience and behaviour? I cannot rule that out but feel on the whole that making more sense of their experience was without exception described as helpful. Several women said that they had initially signed up to the interviews because they wanted to be of help with my research, but then found the interviews were surprisingly helpful for themselves.

PART III
SUMMARY AND CONCLUSION

When starting to research the subject of weddings I was not at all sure where this would lead me. I knew I wanted to make sense of my own at times puzzling experience of my child's wedding, but it was the fact that so many women I had spoken with informally seemed to be equally confused about what their role was and how they felt about it that made me wonder whether I was on to something that may be of interest to more people. As a result, I decided to conduct more formal interviews with mothers of brides and grooms.

I interviewed twenty-five women whose children were about to get married. I spoke with them soon after the announcement of the engagement, then again at some stage during the wedding preparation and, for a last time, after the wedding. This amounted to over one hundred hours of interview material, and gradually a shape to their stories emerged.

With all the wedding interviews now done, having listened to so many mothers' different stories and traced the similarities between them as well as the differences, where does that leave us? All those strong feelings, all those puzzling reactions: what *is* it all about and how can we make sense of it?

1) Weddings as a family rite of passage

Maybe it is important to state the obvious first: weddings are ritual markers of change. They are one of the last remaining rites of passage for families in our society. What does that mean?

A rite of passage is generally defined as a ceremony of a passage which occurs to mark an individual's move from one group to another, involving a change of status, bringing with it a changed sense of identity and changed relationships with significant people around them. Weddings in all cultures mark such a change, signifying the couple entering a new phase of adulthood and a redrawing of boundaries as far as their families of origin are concerned. What became increasingly visible to me is the fact that this rite of passage does not just mark a significant change for the wedding couple, but also for their families. Both sets of families have to incorporate a new member into their family and tolerate their own child joining another family. The wedding marks the fact that they will no longer be the same families that they once were and that brings with it tasks of adaptation and feelings associated with it.

All the women I interviewed were aware of the fact that this wedding marked a significant change in their families. Even if this change itself may have in practice been well established, in that the wedding couple may have been together and lived together for a while, the fact that they were now getting married is experienced as making a substantial difference. The ritual of the wedding focuses the attention on this change and most of the women I spoke with engaged in thinking backwards and forwards in tune with the function of the rite of passage.

2) Family stretchmarks

The main function of the wedding ritual as a rite of passage for the family is to mark a point of restructuring and change in the original definition of family for both families. The family of origin is being extended and its boundaries are being stretched, accommodating from now on not only a new member, the son/daughter-in-law, but also having to process the fact that there are now overlapping family ties: their own son/daughter is joining another family, and the parents themselves may have to engage in a still-to-be-defined and unpredictable relationship with their child's in-laws. It is interesting that there are no linguistic terms in English and most European languages describing what kind of kinship relationship the two sets of parents have with each other. The two mothers can only describe each other's position indirectly with reference to the next generation (my son's/daughter's mother-in-law or my son-in-law's/daughter-in-law's mother). The Spanish "co Madre" and "co Padre" are an exception in that they describe the relationship directly. The more common lack of linguistic term for this relationship indicates a confusion in Western culture about the nature of this new relationship.

If weddings as rites of passage are placed right at the pivotal point between the family in its original shape and the family in its new extended shape, then they may also serve as a focal point and trigger for feelings that are provoked by the tasks of adaptation that accompany this transition. My own professional background is in psychology and psychotherapy and, looking at weddings and the transition in a family that is marked by them, I began to be reminded of something that I was more familiar with, namely the emotional and psychological tasks involved in stretching the family boundaries in other contexts when a new member or new members have to be accommodated: the arrival of a baby, for example, an event that makes a couple into parents, creating grandparents, uncles, aunts, brothers and sisters, with the adjustments involved for all participants.

Then there are events like the formation of step families and adoptive families. Here, just as in weddings, the families of origin are undergoing a substantial change and have to renegotiate the boundaries of their family systems and accommodate a new member into the existing family system. Each time roles, rules and subsystems in a family undergo a change which generates at least a temporary imbalance. The success of this process seems to depend hugely on the family's levels of stability and adaptability, the family's "pre-crisis" functioning and the levels of support available. It seems important to "give up the dream" and *fantasy* of the new family, and rather acknowledge the *reality* of the new family and its complicated and often, at least initially, conflicted quality.

The tasks presented to a family by the change symbolised by a wedding do not differ substantially from the tasks facing a family in the adoption and stepfamily scenarios. They demand a renegotiation of external boundaries around the family and of internal relationships within the family. This process of renegotiation is difficult enough as it is, but is made even more so by the fact that there will be members of the family system who may not have wanted this change or who feel that they have little control over it.

In fact, the pressures and undercurrents that characterise the stretching and re-shaping of family boundaries and the clash between fantasy and reality that accompany weddings are arguably more visible when looking at the parents of the wedding couple rather than at the young couple itself. Parents of both bride and groom are involved in this event to different degrees, often financially, often in terms of organising and planning the event, but without exception this is an event that has an emotional impact on them. They are however not any more in control of the wedding event, as they may have been a couple of generations ago, but are very much at the receiving end of the emotional fallout of the reshaping of their family.

There was no doubt in the interviews that this was how mothers saw what was happening: whether they liked their new son-in-law or daughter-in-law or not, whether they got on with the other family or not, they were on the receiving end of decisions made by somebody else. The fact that most decisions regarding the wedding were made by the wedding couple, and not any more by their parents, mirrored this. Again, most mothers agreed that this is how it should be. Most of them knew and were able to explore the fact that this is not the whole story: thinking that something is right does not mean you cannot have mixed feelings about it, and sure enough they had!

3) Weddings and loss and conflict

I have already identified the potential of weddings to tell us something about a family's dealing with the potential clash between fantasy and reality. Looking at the research into the formation of step families and adoptive families drew my attention to a more specific parallel, namely how the experience of loss, separation and conflict is handled in the families concerned.

Loss is particularly visible in the mother's experience of her child's wedding. Are they really "not losing a daughter but gaining a son" or vice versa? What is clear is that the wedding marks a change in their relationship with their child, whose primary relationship from now on will officially be with their partner and not with their parent any more. Of course, the wedding is not creating this change, but it is in its ritual confirming and marking it.

There was no question about loss figuring in the interviews. Some mothers easily identified it as an aspect of their experience; for others it was more in the background. It came up as early as in the first interviews after the announcement of the engagement; it ran through the preparation stage where it was present particularly in mothers reflecting on their diminishing role in their child's life, as symbolised in various aspects of the wedding preparations; and it was very visible on the day. In the preparation stage it was the confusion over the role the mother might have at the wedding as hostess or as special or not-so-special guest that provided a focus for comparing present and past and the loss of one's position at the centre of one's child's life. All the women in the interviews were aware that this process is part of being a parent and had been going on through all their years of being a mother. They knew that this was how it should be and yet now around the wedding they had to notice it again and feel it again. At the wedding itself it was especially the experience of the stepping back part of the ritual that highlighted this loss again, yet for most mothers, particularly those who had been aware of it and had been able to reflect on it, this was now an emotional but also often a joyful moment.

If loss was visible, then so was a particular family's way of dealing with conflict. Decisions had to be made about aspects of the wedding, such as finances, venues, invitations, seating plans, type of ceremony etc. At each point there was the potential for a clash between what the different people involved may want and how they were or were not involved in the negotiations. All this was acted out against the background of styles of conflict management within a particular family, but also involved the new task of having to take into account another family and their style. Again, mothers knew about this, and their stories are full of details of such conflict and their feelings about it.

4) Weddings and the taboo on negative feelings

As the literature on stepfamilies and adoption suggests, a taboo on awareness and acknowledgement of such undercurrents of loss and conflict can block a successful working through of these feelings and connections within the families. This is equally relevant for weddings. It leads us to another point: if weddings are rites of passage for the whole family, denoting a restructuring and reshaping of the original family that brings with it tasks of adaptation, including dealing with loss and conflict, then that presents the participants with an additional problem: the increased pressure of the dream and fantasy of the perfect day, marketed by the wedding industry and embraced by popular culture, but also adopted in the imaginings of the family and the couple, allows no room for potentially negative and troubling feelings. If they are there, they are often seen to represent failure, and clash with the wish to present oneself and one's family to the public eye. After all, weddings are public events.

It is interesting that my initial title for this book, "Family Stretchmarks", was found by many to be too negative and had associations with something one might want to hide and not talk about. This is precisely why it appealed to me: just like pregnancies, weddings and their preparations have the function of preparing for something new involving a process of emotional stretching, as described in this book, that can indeed involve something that all participants are slightly embarrassed about and might want to hide. However, given the amount of preparation, financial and emotional investment, the day has to be the perfect celebration. Indeed, it was repeatedly suggested to me to change the nature of the book to one that gives helpful advice: how to achieve this perfect celebration, perfect not just as an event, but perfect in its emotional build-up and experience. It is this idea that, if we try hard enough, perfection is after all an option, and if we don't manage it this must be somehow our own fault. As a result, there is a huge taboo on acknowledging or expressing the more complicated emotional undercurrents

This was noticeable in my interviews. Most mothers were wanting to present themselves and their families as easy going and coping well with this wedding. There might be difficult weddings, but not for them and their family. Indeed, there were of course some weddings that seemed to move from engagement to wedding day without too much stress or distress. However, what was equally noticeable, was that some mothers found it easier than others to explore feelings that did not fit so easily the perfect wedding and perfect family scenario. This was clearly not just a question of these mothers having a more difficult time with the wedding, but rather it seemed more related to some of them finding it easier to tolerate the notion of mixed feelings; maybe they were less threatened by exploring the lack of "perfection" in their family and in the wedding.

It seemed to me that the elation that some of them experienced when the day was finally over and had gone well, had partly to do with this: there *had* been difficulties, they had to work their way through them, and by the time the wedding took place a lot of work had been done that had nothing to do with caterers and flower arrangements, but was emotional work. In fact it could be argued that this is precisely the function of wedding "stress", namely forcing the participants to work through some of the issues that the wedding represents.

5) Weddings and the family as it was: looking back

One mother I talked to described the time of the wedding preparations of her daughter as an "unparalleled experience". Whilst of course this comment tries to capture the extraordinariness of events and their rather unexpected and "strange" nature, I would like to challenge the notion of lack of parallels. In fact, I think quite the opposite is true. The maternal experience of their child's wedding may indeed have a number of highly relevant parallels in the life of the family and the individual woman's life. Whatever each of these mothers would have learned before about how to deal with similar events, similar in that they would also involve dealing not only with separation, loss, rivalry, but also sharing and letting go, she would now somehow have to access it again. The weddings seemed to stir up these experiences, triggering old feelings and established coping strategies.

My point is that, when coping with the emotional tasks that the transition symbolised by a wedding presents family members with, each of them are likely to use coping strategies that are specific to this particular family and this particular person. Whatever they have learned about how to cope with change and loss, they are going to use again to meet this new challenge. All the women I interviewed seemed to be engaged in some looking back and looking forward at this crucial juncture of their lives and the lives of their family, as the conceptualisation of weddings as a family rite of passage suggests.

They looked back on their family as they remembered them as mothers of this particular child. Other formative experiences in the specific history of a mother and her child regarding earlier stages of separation and the child's move towards independence away from Mother came up and I encouraged my interviewees to think about them. How did they experience times like when the child started school, when they became adolescents and when they left home? How much was that separation and leaving home threatening the identity of the mother? Did she feel lost and without purpose, or sad but also eventually liberated and free to pursue her own identity? Did the child manage an identity separate and away from the parent? Do mother and child sound secure and comfortable in that separate identity or do they sound still merged with too little space between them? Have both parties managed to share with each other whilst maintaining boundaries? Have they developed significant relationships away from each other and tolerated and enjoyed this extension of their relationship? Is there such a thing as a specific "style" of separation that is being repeated here in the wedding preparation? Does the experience of separation highlight regrets and guilt over the pre-separation quality of the relationship? All these questions came up in the interviews, sometimes in direct accounts, sometimes only visible behind the story.

Beyond that I asked mothers to also look back at their own story as a child or young adult in their family of origin. Were they able to successfully separate from their own parents? Did this separation lead to satisfactory or unsatisfactory new adult relationships with parents, siblings and possibly new in-law families? Expectations will have been created for each woman as to how families merge successfully or fail to do so. Were grandparents a part of the family? Were both sets of grandparents part of the family and how was that experienced? Was the mother's own partner accepted into the family and did he or she make an effort to be part of the family? Were there experiences of sisters-in-law, brothers-in-law, uncles' and aunts' partners "taking away" the blood relative? Were both sets of family kept apart or mixed and how? All these experiences will set the scene for expectations, hopes and fears regarding this new situation of the child marrying into another family.

These past experiences clearly did colour the current experience of the wedding, as both the general themes emerging throughout the interviews and particularly the individual stories in Chapter 4 show. Patterns of behaviour relating to this particular child and the quality of the moving towards separation and independence involved in bringing up this child played a huge part in the story of the wedding. Mothers had to use what they had learned as mothers of this child and as an adult with their own specific childhood history. They needed to deal with this event that has at its centre the parents stepping back from the child. They needed to celebrate their child's move towards their partner as their main significant other, and towards the other family as a group with an equal claim on the new couple as their family. If parenting involves a series of moves required from the parents that involves stepping back, then here it is played out again in front of an audience and full of emotional charge. Many of the difficult moments for mothers were associated with the stepping back, but were perhaps more difficult when conditions did not soften this experience. What clearly made the biggest difference was their being sufficiently reassured that they still mattered to their child in spite of having to step back: in other words to trust that relationships can survive separation and change.

6) Weddings and the family as it will be: looking forward

Rites of passage point backwards and forwards and a crucial aspect of weddings is that they indicate the direction of travel for the families involved. In fact, it could be said that the majority of upsets at weddings, or during the time of their preparations, have to do with this fact. Does it really matter where the wedding is being held, who is involved in the preparations, who sits where and who is mentioned in the invitations? What became clear to me in the interviews is that it does indeed matter, the reason being that these details are felt to have the potential to point ahead. The wedding is after all an event that is shared by two more or less extended families who will both claim the new couple as part of their family. With it appear questions of rivalry and territorial claim, sometimes very close to the surface, sometimes more hidden, but inevitably present. The question of which family is more involved or more in charge of the wedding is more complicated these days, because old rules that stated the dominance of the family of the bride hardly apply any more. It is the couple who tend on the whole to make most of the decisions concerning details of the wedding, so involving or not involving their families is an act that is not any more governed by tradition, but rather indicates where the couple place themselves in relation to their respective families. This may be experienced by the mothers as appropriate independence and an indication of their child's maturity. However, there is always the potential for feeling excluded, particularly if the other family is seen to be more included.

This is why the notion of generosity that I came across in many interviews seemed to play such a big part. Mothers see their child as being in charge and they are on the whole happy with this if they feel their child is generous and allowing them to be included. If that is not the case, feelings of loss, hurt and jealousy become bigger and, above all, there is fear that this is the shape of things to come. For me the idea of becoming the "Boxing Day family", as one mother put it, sums this up rather neatly. The new couple will decide which family comes first and which will be second: that is the subtext for many mothers' concerns. Family therapists often ask their clients to draw a picture of the family and they find information in how this is done. How close are family members to each other in those drawings? What is their relative size? Who is at the centre or at the margins of the picture? I think weddings have a similar communicative potential for depicting where all participants stand in relationship to each other right now, and, more importantly, where they may stand in the future.

If not being a hostess any more may indicate a loss of a past role for the mother concerned, then not being a special enough guest scares them for the future. The child's refusal to mark his or her alliance with the family of origin creates the "Boxing Day" scenario, where the fear is that the link to the family of origin may just become progressively weaker, with the other family being seen as a potential rival. This is why questions concerning who knows first about the engagement, who is involved in the planning, or even who is mentioned on the invitation, and above all where the wedding is going be held and which family has the associated "territorial advantage", matter so much. Mothers of grooms have to face this in general more clearly around the wedding preparations, as brides and their mothers in many cases still do the majority of the wedding work. However, their position normalises this to an extent and they can at least present this to the outside world without feeling that this indicates some kind of failure. Mothers of brides who feel the other family are in the more dominant position seem to feel this much more acutely. For either group any confirmation of the link between their child and them makes other details of the day fade in significance, as the accounts in Chapter 3 show. The most "successful" weddings were characterised by a strongly felt and expressed connection between mother and child and a warm reaching out from the dominant to the less dominant family, mainly of course the new son-in-law or daughter-in-law, but followed closely by the relationship that developed between the two mothers. If those factors are in place, then a sharing with the other family becomes a possibility. Generosity creates generosity. If it is not present, then things are more difficult. The tasks of coping with change, loss and rivalry are however not just a characteristic of the more difficult weddings, but are present in all of them.

Family stretchmarks?

The more I have heard, read and understood about weddings, the more I feel that my original title made an important point. Stretchmarks are associated with a physical aspect of pregnancy. As mothers, we may be left with them long after the child has been born, reminding us how our body had to stretch to accommodate the growing child inside us. A truly creative process, no doubt, leading to a momentous event that will change our life and that of our families forever: the birth of a child and becoming a mother. This process involves enormous physical and emotional changes. Stretchmarks tell this story and they remind us of a price we had to pay: our bodies are not the same anymore and there may be aspects of this that we are unhappy about and may want to hide.

For me there are clear parallels to what it is about weddings that creates such complicated emotions. Here it is not our bodies that are being stretched, but our families and how we have defined them, our relationship with our child and how we have defined this. Pregnancy leads a woman towards the event of the birth of her child and gives her at the same time the chance to gradually prepare emotionally to accommodate this new person into her life. Here too, the pressure to have one-dimensional feelings, to be unambiguously excited about the pregnancy and to be equally unambiguously looking forward to becoming a mother, is enormous. Can the pregnant woman give herself permission to acknowledge ambivalent feelings? What if there is fear about the future, or resentment of this little alien taking over one's body, or loss and grief at seeing one's life and one's body change, the stretchmarks telling this story? Something similar is happening around weddings: mothers are under pressure to have one-dimensional feelings, and feel embarrassed about the emotional stretchmarks they are left with in this process of accommodating the extension of their family and the stretching of the emotional umbilical cord between their child and themselves. Ambivalent feelings must be hidden and the illusion of the possibility of the perfect wedding and the perfect family must be maintained. The result is, however, isolation and the sense that everybody else manages this without stretchmarks, or that at least it would be possible to do so, if only one could get hold of the right manual. Stretchmarks become an indication of failure and shame.

If there is one conclusion I have taken from these interviews and their analysis, then it is this:

Weddings are stressful. This is normal and it is part of the work that needs to be done in order to manage change. It is not an indication of failure, but rather part of a creative process that family life with its constant demand for change brings with it. Understanding the meaning of this stressful stretching process, rather than chasing the illusion that it can somehow be avoided, seems to me the most helpful and productive response.

Acknowledgements

First and foremost my thanks go to all the mothers who agreed to be interviewed and who generously shared their experiences with me.

I would also like to thank colleagues and friends who offered me their time in reading and re-reading the manuscript, giving me invaluable comments, advice and encouragement. I would like to mention my clinical supervisor Gillian Isaacs Russell, Patrick Stevenson who helped me in matters of interview research, but also friends and "maternal experts" Christine Bunday, Lucy Cooper, Elizabeth Marks, Jeanne Moulton, Fiona Thompson, and above all Wendy Gracias who did not tire when she may well have done!

Alice Solomons from FAB was clear, prompt and helpful in her communications and made my experience of working with a publisher a very easy and rewarding one.

Thanks to Anna, Chris, Kate and Sam who listened and encouraged.

In particular thanks to John for his patience and support, as always.